THE PROPHET ELIJAH

"And behold, two men talked with Him, Moses and Elijah, who appeared in glory"
Luke 9:30-31

Also by Barbara Fleming:

The Fishermen of Jesus. Diadem Books.

Three Men in a Book: Heroes of the Bible. Diadem Books.

Your Path to the Kingdom. Diadem Books.

Hooray! We Have Found the Holy Spirit! Diadem Books.

Hooray! We Have Found the Kingdom! Diadem Books.

Hooray! We have found our Hero (General Gordon). Memoirs Publishing.

We Escaped to the Country: And it Rained Cats & Dogs – and Donkeys. Memoirs Publishing

Welcome! To the Joy of Christianity! Diadem Books.

"I Am The Light of the World." Diadem Books.

The Prophet Elijah. Diadem Books.

My Servant Paul. Diadem Books.

THE PROPHET ELIJAH

by

Barbara Fleming

DB

DIADEM BOOKS

THE PROPHET ELIJAH

All Rights Reserved. Copyright © 2014 Barbara Fleming

No part of this book may be reproduced or transmitted in any form or by any means, graphic, electronic, or mechanical, including photocopying, recording, taping or by any information storage or retrieval system, without the permission in writing from the copyright holder.

The right of Barbara Fleming to be identified as the author of this work has been asserted in accordance with the Copyright, Designs and Patents Act 1988 sections 77 and 78.

Published by Diadem Books

For information, please contact:
Diadem Books
16 Lethen View
ALLOA
FK10 2GE
Scotland UK
www.diadembooks.com

The views expressed in this work are solely those of the author and do not necessarily reflect the views of the publisher, and the publisher hereby disclaims any responsibility for them.

ISBN: 978-1-326-01380-6

CONTENTS

Foreword

Chapter

1. ELIJAH AND AHAB
2. ELIJAH AND THE RAVENS
3. THE WIDOW OF ZAREPHATH
4. MOUNT CARMEL
5. JEZEBEL THE QUEEN
6. THE STILL SMALL VOICE
7. ELISHA
8. ELIJAH RETURNS
9. THE BATTLE OF APHEK AND NABOTH'S VINEYARD
10. ELIJAH IN ISRAEL AND THE DEATH OF AHAB
11. KING AHAZIAH
12. ELIJAH'S FINAL JOURNEY

AFTERWORD

FOREWORD

AFTER 400 YEARS IN EGYPT the Israelites re-settled in Canaan. They became a united nation, finally a Kingdom! But, following three noteworthy rulers, sadly the Kingdom split to become Israel in the north and Judah in the south.

Then a second nightmare of evil spread swiftly across the northern Kingdom ruled now by a King Ahab, centred on the city of Samaria. He had wed the daughter of the pagan neighbouring King of Syria and the pagan worship of Baal, as a malicious darkness, had entered the land with the new queen Jezebel. In her train she had brought "four hundred and fifty prophets" of her pagan God, raising a splendid temple for them in Samaria. The worship of the One True God was mercilessly outlawed and all the priests of it hounded into death or hiding. A tragedy that the Lord God must have looked down upon with a penetrating grief.

But as He had in the beginning, when He had chosen only one single individual, Abraham, to bring light and truth to the Earth, He now assigned one humble, faithful follower to become the man to save His people. In doing so, the chosen man would become the greatest prophet of all time—Elijah!

Again, as with Jacob, as we study his life from then on, we find there was much hardship to overcome in the years ahead as Elijah fought the battle of his God, and again, as it was with Jacob, we can truly learn much from it to encourage and guide ourselves in our own struggles in life. Above all we can learn a trust and strength to overcome adversity in the love and power of our triumphant Lord God.

Elijah was a "real man" and now may we read on and rejoice in his "overcoming" as he faithfully followed the leading of his One True God to work His will in our World.

Chapter 1

ELIJAH AND AHAB

OVER THE HILLS OF ISRAEL the olives ripened lazily in the heat. Above them the new town of Samaria sprawled, languid over honey-coloured slopes, a fine, new capital and symbol of the solid power of the House of Omri, rulers of the land. From the palace walls the clamour of trumpets shattered the golden peace:
"The King has sacrificed!"
"The Baals receive the royal sacrifice!"
"Hail to our king, Ahab the Mighty!"
"Hail to our queen, the gracious Jezebel!"

The gates swung wide as the hot sand spattered up from hoof and chariot wheel. Inside the courtyard Obadiah vaulted down to receive the Royalty descending. The horses freed, he clattered them with expert handling across the palace yard. Marvellous animals, they reined in, snorting and sweating in the heat, before the gateway to the palace stables.

The giant doors dragged back, etching two wide arcs in the sand. The horses thudded through. Obadiah's eyes followed his charges as they were led away into the shaded stalls. Turning at the greeting of

Esiah, Keeper of the Royal Stables, his face exploded with contempt.

"Pah! The smell of dung and stable straw comes a deal cleaner to my nostrils than the rancid incense of those screeching priests!" Esiah's touch on his wrist warned him to caution. "Have a care," he murmured. "The Queen's ears, they say these days, come as sharp as her jewelled claws."

"And as sharp as the knives of her priest-butchers I've no doubt. Never fear, my friend, I can hold my tongue before the Peacock's throne. Give me a flagon of cold wine, Esiah, to clear the taste of it all out of my gullet."

Their voices were swallowed up into the cavern of the guard-room.

Obadiah flung himself wearily down. A servant materialised out of the darkness holding a bowl of water. The Israelite plunged his arms in, elbow deep.

"Ah, your cold wine is good, Esiah, but your icy water is even better, thanks be to the God of Abraham, father of well-diggers, eh?"

"You are safe here, at least, to praise Him if nowhere else within the palace walls. How does the Court?"

"Like pigs as usual, I've no doubt, tearing and guzzling at the feast and ravenous as the Baal after the long hours in attendance on their Majesties before the altars in this heavy sun."

"Baal take the lot of them!"

"Give me clean horses nosing an honest feed-bowl in their stalls. There's good sense in that, now, and dignity as well."

Esiah nodded, relieved to turn the talk through safer channels with servants still at hand. "Aye, the King values his horses as the jewels in his treasure house… Now try the roast yearling, my lord. You'll find it goes well with the wine of Jezreel…"

Outside all became quiet except for the graceful flicking of a tail or the comfortable shuffling of a set of hooves. The sand had been immaculately re-raked, the wooden gates were shut and, while the two friends quietly talked and ate, the royal stables of Samaria fell asleep through the drowsy afternoon.

Esiah dismissed the slaves and poured more wine. "Now we can talk safely, Obadiah. Tell me first, how did you find the followers of the one true God of Israel?"

"Holed up in caves like frightened sheep now that the Gods of Jezebel, Baal and Ashtaroth, stalk across the land."

"Baal," Esiah spat. "And all the gods of Sidon! A palace he builds, our king, set like a crown upon this hill and now he lets that witch Jezebel rear up a temple to a foul moon goddess right beside it. I tell you, Obadiah, it looks more like a vulture sitting there, brooding and thirsting for our blood, the blood of Israel."

"Ah, a bad day for Israel when our Ahab wed the King of Sidon's daughter."

Esiah remonstrated, "It was all for trade. But what a country he has made of us though, rich and powerful! And his building! I'll swear the walls of Meggido and Hazor will outlast the stones in Solomon's temple there in Jerusalem. He may prove an even finer builder than his father yet. Look at Samaria here and this Ivory Palace!"

"I wonder if they *will* outlast the Temple in Jerusalem?" mused Obadiah. "At least there the altars are cleaner of sacrilege and the God of Abraham is still praised openly. The wisdom of Solomon still keeps the people of the Southern Kingdom faithful."

"A pity," retorted Esiah. "He was not wise enough to leave the Chosen People a united country. Too busy with his building and his wives, I reckon. A bit more wisdom and our Israel would not have had to break away and become this Northern Kingdom as it is. We would still have been united as the good Samuel intended when he chose a king to rule God's People in their Promised Land."

Obadiah yawned lazily. "No good flogging that dead horse, my friend. We're divided and the House of Omri rules us Northerners and Jezebel rules the House of Omri."

"You're right," agreed Esiah. "And what could be more pleasant than sitting here, in the guard-room of

King Ahab's stables, sleepily putting the world to rights over his finest wines?"

The shadows lengthened across the city. A first breeze ruffled the water in the stone drinking troughs.

Back in the palace an army of servants began to pick their way silently between the lines of snoring courtiers, clearing the debris of the feast, spreading fresh rushes on the marble floors and flinging wide the curtains. Through the courtyard there came the first murmuring of the advancing crowd of petitioners to the Late Noon Audience. Reluctantly Obadiah stretched his legs and hauled himself to his feet.

"Listen to the buzzing of the human locusts mustering in the forecourt. Bees to the honey-pot of Ahab. Well, I must go and watch their grovelling backsides, I suppose, and listen to the gobbling of their pleas."

"You grow cynical at the Ivory Court. Surely some of them come with genuine petitions or even worthy gifts?"

"Aye, there'll be a sprinkling of over-proud freemen, I've no doubt, and even a handful of clear-eyed merchants from Tarshish or beyond. But for the rest, they'll bring a good rich stink of mutton fat and a pocketful of fleas to accompany their grovelling and flattery, you'll see.

That young chap Jehu, he has a good way with handling them. Seems to be able to sort the sheep out from the goats on sight… or maybe he uses his nose, eh?"

The jest improved his humour as he stepped through the postern gate and made his way towards the palace. The anterooms were already crowded, but he threaded his way through the sea of hopeful hands and anxious faces with a skill born of long practice. Only just in time, he reached the throne-room before the trumpets of the heralds cut through the hum of voices and drew all eyes to the royal entrance. In the moment of hush that followed the last strident note the splendid figure of King Ahab swept into the room and strode up to his throne of ivory.

He turned a swarthy, hawk-like face to acknowledge the shuffling and the cowering around the hall and then he paused, erect, while his purple robe was draped with deference to his satisfaction. Seating himself with the assured indifference of royalty, he assumed an intent expression with his eyes fixed upon the massive doors at the far end of the room.

By an unspoken order every face revolved to focus, with his, in the same direction.

Obadiah felt his pulse thumping that much faster. There was a thrill of anticipation in the air. Always it was like this. First the king made his grand approach and then… they waited, like well-trained curs Obadiah thought, until the quickest ears picked up the rustle of approaching silks.

Then at last the doors would swing open as if by magic, and there, framed in the doorway, would stand the dazzling arrogance of Queen Jezebel.

Princess of Phoenicia and Queen to the Throne of Israel, she stood still in her entrance savouring, like incense, the essence of the servility she commanded.

The charge of her personality electrified the room. Exhilaration, laced with fear, rippled over the bowing, bobbing heads. Her eyes, aloof, sought those of the King and met and linked with his in a triumph private to themselves.

Almost against his will Obadiah's eyes were drawn upwards to her face. Her straight hair, raven black, outlined the perfection of her brow and high cheekbones. Her finely cosmeticised eyes shone with dark excitement. Her blood-red mouth echoed the flaring crimson of her robes, vibrant and luscious.

As she moved towards the thrones she passed within arm's length of him and his nostrils stung with a wave of her exotic perfume. Yet he sensed something almost snake-like in her glide across the marble tiles. She took her seat with elegance and grace, but the curve of her slim fingers, talon-like over the ivory arm-rests, ran a cold spice of fear down his spine. He shivered.

Blaringly the trumpets scattered his imaginings. The King had signalled, "Let the Audience begin!"

The call for the first petitioner repeated itself down through the anteroom:

"Japhet, merchant of Ezion-Geber, stand forth. His majesty is pleased to hear your suit... Japhet, merchant... Japhet"...

Finally the man appeared. He entered warily, clearly overawed by the armour of the guards and all the surrounding splendour. At last he found his voice to plead:

"Most royal and excellent sovereign... Exalted Graciousness..." As he lisped his humbleness his fingers were pulling feverishly at the cords that tied his bundles. Suddenly the strapping gave and his wares showered in a stream of blazing colour across the marble steps. A rainbow of silks shimmered through his hands. Over them his dark face, pointed and anxious, peered up at the Queen, ever hopeful... The next... and then the next...

Gems sparkled, jewelled belts writhed like golden serpents from their baskets. Slippers of softest leather tempted the royal touch, carpets from Arabia, ivory from the land of Phut, unguents, spices, silver...

"Most royal and excellent One..."

"Great seed of the mighty Omri..."

So the voices droned on, each rivalling the last with its oil of flattery.

Finally, bored with this surfeit of sumptuousness, Obadiah amused himself by watching the way that Jehu marshalled the long queue. His eye wandered down the line to the latest arrival between the high entrance pillars.

Here was one for sure of whom Jehu would make short shrift—a wild-looking creature and, unless that pouch of his hid gold nuggets, empty-handed too except for his knotted staff.

Perhaps it was the look of the staff that reminded Obadiah of the figure of Moses daring to approach the Egyptian Pharaoh's throne.

"Great heavens, he must have had too much of that Jezreel wine!"

He brushed away his fancies, but still he found his eyes kept going back again and resting on the uncouth figure with his tangled hair and weather-beaten face.

Strange about his face! He looked like someone almost walking in his sleep. He moved along the line like someone in a dream.

Obadiah heard the herald's voice, prompted by Jehu:

"Eli of Jericho..." and then, "Elijah the Tishbite!"

Suddenly the chamber went quiet as the silent figure of Elijah, not bowing but erect, stood in the lonely space before the thrones.

Obadiah's eyes flickered to Jehu. To his amazement he saw that young soldier gravely at attention, a look almost of reverence upon his face. He returned his gaze to Ahab and steeled himself to withstand the searing blast of royal wrath.

Instead the voice of Elijah the Tishbite rang through the court:

"The Lord, the God of Israel liveth! Blessed be His Holy Name!"

The King sat frozen on his seat. The Audience chamber held its breath.

"Hear, O Israel, the word of the Lord your God!

You, King Ahab, have you not raised up an abomination in My House, saith the Lord? Have you not bowed down to the Baals of Sidon brought to you by your queen? Are My altars not fouled with their bloody sacrifice?

Lechery and sodomy plague My Holy Places! The hills are crowned with your lusts and the valleys flow with the lifeblood of My Faithful! You have turned away from the God of Abraham, the God of Isaac and the God of Jacob and led My children into whoredom!" Like an avenging angel he raised his arms high above his head. Then down they came, his staff striking the tiles like the crack of doom.

"Woe unto you Ahab, King of Israel! Woe unto you, Queen Jezebel of Sidon! Hear now the judgement of the Lord your God!"

He flung his words directly at the thrones. The chamber waited, spellbound.

"Now for your betrayal of Him and for your fearful works before the altars of the alien gods, thus has the Lord our God ordained: That there shall be no drop of rain or dew nor any moisture fall upon this land until your sin is purged and as I shall command it at His word!"

He stopped as abruptly as he had begun.

The King, his face livid with anger, was on his feet,

"Stop, I say! Seize hold the traitor! Put him in chains! Out with his lying tongue!"

The spell was broken and a storm of noise swelled in an instant to an uproar.

"Sound the alarm!"

"Treason! Hold the doors!"

Elijah's fate seemed sealed. But not by Ahab! Suddenly the place before the thrones was empty.

Jehu's place was empty too…

Chapter 2

ELIJAH AND THE RAVENS

OBADIAH'S SHARP EYES searched the crowded room. He frowned in disbelief. Where was the man?

One moment he had stood there, thundering before the throne. Now, just as terrifyingly, he had disappeared into thinnest air.

But what of his dreadful prophecy? "No drop of rain nor any dew." Here was horror indeed.

No drop of rain would mean no growth of pasture, and no pasture would spell death in agony to all those splendid beasts he loved as his own children.

Had the wrath of the God of Jacob grown so fierce it must be measured thus in fear and cruelty?

It was all the doing of that witch Jezebel. He cursed her under his breath and all her two-faced priests, driving them to disaster such as this. No rain! He shuddered. God help them all and curses on the Queen and all her Baals again!

"Out of my way!" bellowed the guard, forcing him aside. "The man Elijah, where did he go? After him, I say!"

"Oh, devil take you and Elijah!" Obadiah swore back at him. "Ask the God of Israel where he is. He brought him here, to curse us all to hell." And spirited him away, it seemed, as mysteriously as He had caused him to appear, leading him, at the swift beckoning of Jehu, into the maze of subterranean tunnels that burrowed beneath the palace. "Come master, only another turn or two and you are safe for sure," he urged.

Elijah followed him unseeing.

"Did you hear what the Lord said, Jehu? Did you hear Him speaking through me or did I dream it?"

"No master, He spoke right enough. Like the thunder on the mountains came His voice, storming against the gods of Jezebel."

"It came upon me in the cave where we were hiding, over by Shechem. 'Elijah, will you speak for me?' it said. I thought it just my fancy but it came again. 'Elijah, will you speak for me? Will you be the trumpet for the Lord?' I was aghast. You know I am such a tongue-tied thing. What use could I be as a trumpet?

'There's Elochim now, Lord, he has a marvellous flow of words. Or Jachel or Zephoria, they would…' But it came again. I could not shut it out.

'I have chosen you, Elijah, to be the champion of the God of Israel. You I choose to be my sword. Go to the court of Ahab. Trust Me and go!'

So at last I went." His forehead creased. "But where is the Power that walked with me, Jehu, and kept me in such a tower of safe assurance? As soon as I had spoken I felt it suddenly drain away. Surely the Lord could have chosen a much braver, better man than I?"

"Courage, my lord."

"Not 'lord', Jehu. Not to me. Not as you love me."

"Yes, lord Elijah. For now you are the Chosen One and, even if the power has gone for now, I cannot believe the Lord our God will leave you unshielded. Tonight we shall see you out of Samaria and on your way by the sheep-tracks over Jordan and into Gilead. You must know a likely valley somewhere there, where you can stay unnoticed for a time." He looked shrewdly at the figure beside him.

"You know, master, when you think of it, the Lord God has a habit of taking His chosen ones into the wilderness. The wild places were ever the schoolroom of His wisdom. Methinks if there is to be a battle royal between our God and their majesties of Israel, we need time to learn the tactics of our General. Now He has thrown the challenge down and fixed the fight, He surely intends that we should turn aside and look to our weapons and our means before the action comes in earnest."

Days later, gaunt and weary, Elijah crossed the Jordan into Gilead. Here he was on his own ground and he quickly found a refuge in the hills beside the brook called Cherith where it tumbles its way, in deep and hidden valleys, down to the sacred river.

He sat, hunched and lonely. The sunlight danced and sparkled on the stream, but Elijah was all unseeing of its beauty. For him, even here, the world was still a hot and terrifying place. He who had always loved solitude and quietness now found it strangely threatening.

Then suddenly, out of the nothingness a wondrous reassurance overcame him, stealing up over his feet, his legs, his back. Like a warm wave it soothed away his nightmare fears and fancies, this loving spirit of his Unknown God, and filled his heart with comfort and with peace.

Now at last he saw the sunshine winking at him from the water, felt the softness of the sand and saw the ribbon colours of the rocks and the tiny flowers starring in their crevasses.

Settling back, his thoughts shaped and reshaped themselves over the marvellous happenings of the last few days. Was he really to be the Weapon of the Lord? The Tool of His chastisement? Was it all a dream? And yet, here he was, beside the brook and that was real. How could it be?

By the time that night had fallen his tired brain had wearied itself with thinking and could take no more. With a deep sigh of acceptance he felt for his cloak and, wrapping it tight around him, he curled up, exhausted, on the ground to sleep.

In the morning he awoke chilled and hungry. Looking around he took in his stony surroundings more alertly. His countryman's ears caught at a puzzling sound up there in that cool, free air. A wind? A storm down from the heights? Then out of the wide sky the black specks came wheeling! Soaring down, floating and diving, until their big, flapping wings almost deafened him. Enormous they were, those black ravens, messengers of his God, circling above his head out of the dazzling sunrise. His heart leapt as he saw with wonder how each beak carried a piece of food.

Obedient to their unseen trainer, each raven fearlessly landed and waddled forward to place its offering at Elijah's feet. They looked for all the world, Elijah thought, like a retinue of black slaves attending a king.

Praise and wonder from his heart mounted back into the sky as he watched them sweeping down. Here was indeed the power of his God and he felt the thrill of being one with the wandering chosen people fed on manna in just such a way four hundred years before.

But how they strutted and preened themselves, those gawky birds! How arrogantly they marched off to the stream, to drink, after the meat and bread had been dropped with precision at Elijah's feet! And how they then stood looking at him with those unwinking, beady eyes!

Day after day as they came, Elijah could never quite make up his mind whether they were secretly laughing with him or at him as they waited confidently for the crumbs he threw them as payment for his breakfast and his supper. The trouble was that they all reminded him of Jezebel the Queen!

In spite of his growing trust in God as each morning and each evening came and went, he still remembered how her black eyes had bored her contempt through him as he had stood before the throne. A frightening power of evil had emanated from her, clawing at his throat and trying to throttle him as he spoke.

Then a strange thought struck him. "Could the Almighty make use even of her as His servant as He did these huge, satanic-looking birds? Yet surely we are all of like creation, she and I and the ravens?" He mused and, with that, he was strangely touched by a kind of respect for her strength and for her very determined fight for her convictions, evil though they were.

So the days passed while the Lord God strengthened His lonely servant and melted the dew of His wisdom and compassion drop by drop into Elijah's heart.

But at the same time over Israel, including Gilead beyond Jordan, His curse was slowly drying up the land. Each day the stream lapped a little less closely to the rock against which Elijah sat. Each day the dry ground extended itself yet further into the water. Until there came an evening when there was only a glistening lace of mud left for the ravens to peck at.

Then as they rose, noisy as ever, screeching and flapping over his head, Elijah knew that this had been their last visit to him. His days of quiet in the wilderness were at an end.

Zarephath! That name had kept running through his head these last few days. Zarephath! Did his God direct him there? Zarephath in Sidon? Out of the territory of Israel, for sure, but into the very jaws of Baal!

"Have You forgotten Lord, Jezebel the Queen is daughter to the king of Sidon? Do you send me for my safety to the very fountain source of Baal?"

He shook with fear at the thought.

"Great God" have mercy on me. When You are with me, filling me with Your power and Your spirit, then I am brave. But when You are not within me, Lord, I am a fearful man and weak and trembling. Not to Sidon, Lord, not yet," he pleaded…

But still the thought drummed in his head, "Zarephath, Zarephath. Go Elijah, go!"

He rose off his knees, cast down and puzzled, picked up his stick reluctantly and threw his goatskin cloak around his shoulders. His chin lifted. The light touch of the cloak had brought a comfort to his trembling heart. Somehow he sensed the shield and surety of an extra strength that lay within it now.

"Yes," he thought, "and I shall need it too!" But it was good to feel the Lord God marched with him to Zarephath. Feeling wondrously cheered, he headed out of the hills that had hidden him and down towards the Jordan.

Zarephath lay a long way to the north-west of Gilead and Israel, on the Phoenician coast, midway between the larger towns of Tyre and Sidon. It was a journey of many days on foot from Gilead.

Reaching the Jordan Valley, Elijah turned towards the north and followed the holy river upstream as it idled its leisurely way from the Sea of Chinnereth (now Galilee) down to the dead Sea of Salt.

By day he watched the swifts and sparrows soaring and fluttering above the tamarisks that marked the hidden watercourse. By night he started at the sudden shriek of owls through the darkness and the throaty roar of lions across the empty valley as they prowled the swampy thickets beside the river.

On the third evening he came to the lake and drank thankfully of its ice-cold water.

The Travels of Elijah—Samaria to Carmel

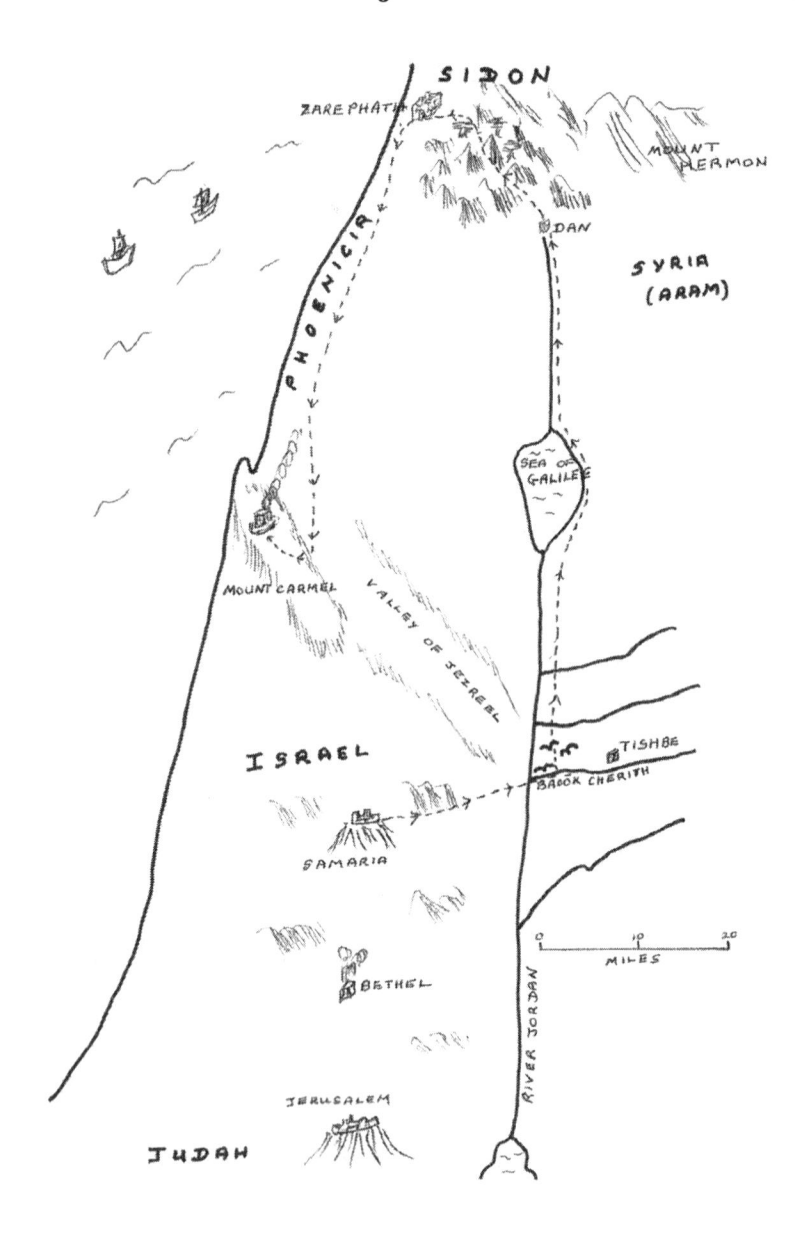

"Where now, Lord? Where do I find the road to Zarephath?" With the first rays of dawn came the answer to his wondering. Away to the north the fingers of early light, brushing the sky with palest pinks deepening to rose and gold, outlined that queen of mountains, crowned with snow, Mount Hermon. It seemed to beckon to Elijah.

"Come," it commanded. "Take up your cloak and staff and follow the path here at my feet. We serve the same Lord God Almighty, you and I, God of Creation, I the mountain of majesty, bow to His overlordship. Your path lies at my feet." The track was rough along the fringes of the Syrian hills, threading through gorges and bare rock to skirt the Jordan basin and the territory of Israel. Night and day continued as Elijah walked, rested, walked again, crawled to the shelter of a cave when the sun rose high, or took to the desolate road once more under a canopy of stars.

Finally he gained the foothills of Mount Hermon. Here, in a hidden valley, he stumbled across one of the headsprings of the sacred river Jordan. This one, inscribed to Ea-Banni the ancient water spirit, he frowned at sternly. A shrine to idols here, at the day-spring of the sacred Jordan? Could this be a hidden sanctuary of the dreaded Baal at the very feet of Hermon? Yet he could see no bloodied slab of sacrifice, no hideous idol stones.

Wondering much he continued on his journey lost in thought. The limestone slopes were spread with ancient cedars sheltering deep valleys luxuriant with greenness. Here too he found the same mysterious worship of the natural forces of the Earth. Each niche and cave sheltered a simple shrine. Yet again there was no atmosphere of evil. Strangely he felt a calm affinity with the place. He sensed a power of growth and rich abundance and goodwill to every living thing, himself included.

This could be no foul fertility worship, distorted by men's minds to feed their lustful passions. This was the pure, primaeval sense of natural fruitfulness.

Thus, without words, another teaching from his God on High revealed itself within his heart. He understood: thus bloomed the Garden of Eden of God's own creation and thus Man came to fall.

Engrossed in his thoughts he was unaware how near his journey was to ending until a sudden blinding change of landscape swept across his view.

Instead of the dappled shade, suddenly there was hot sunlight. The green leafiness of the trees that sheltered him suddenly opened to reveal the sweeping sapphire expanse of the Mediterranean Sea shining to the horizon.

The Phoenician coast! Between the mountains and the beach stretched the flat coastal plain spread rich with orchards, fields and almond groves and towns alive with industry and commerce. It hummed with the clank of metal forging and the splash and thud of dyeing and of tanning.

In the two years that Elijah was to live there he came to know it well. He was to watch as gold and silver, in the fingers of the craftsmen, contorted into a nightmare of strange shapes and images.

He would marvel at the craftsmanship but shudder when he glimpsed the gleaming avarice and hardness reflected in the faces of the craftsmen. Then he would come to understand, only too sadly, how the worship of the nature spirits in the mountains had, in like way, been subject to the twisting, torturing ways of these people of the coast. How a simple reverence and goodness had been cruelly distorted into the worship of the Baal and become the blood-soaked and idolatrous evil with which Jezebel the Queen had poisoned Israel. Here were the traders, the anvil-workers, the grasping adventurers of the ancient world. What use the spirits of the earth to them? Gold was their power, fine skill and bargaining their admiration; and lives could be bought and sold as any merchandise or tossed to feed the hunger of their gods. But for Elijah this was to be a revelation of the days to come. Now, for him, the little town of Zarephath lay almost at his feet and surely his God waited to greet him somewhere there within those walls.

Chapter 3

THE WIDOW OF ZAREPHATH

EXCITEMENT ROSE INSIDE HIM as he picked his way down the mountainside and out across the plain. He was swept along the jostling roads and up to the crowded gateway.

There Elijah paused, uncertain all of a sudden and bewildered by all the bustle and confusion. So many people! And the noise! He had forgotten how busy the world could be.

The chequerboard of awnings scattered over the trading ground in front of the walls was alive with men and women who scurried backwards and forwards almost as frantically as the ants he had watched in the dreamy hours beside the Cherith stream. He stood aloof. The shouting dinned into his ears, merchants struggling to unload their donkeys and eager traders calling out their wares.

Then his eye was caught by a silent woman's figure slipping between the crowds and stooping carefully, every so often, to pick up chippings of wood and broken twigs among the stalls.

Suddenly he realised that, deep inside, he had known all along she would be there…

His eyes followed her as she worked her way around to where he stood and then, her basket filled, she straightened up her back and their eyes met!

Strangely, it seemed to her, as it had to him, that this was what she too had been expecting.

When the prophet spoke his voice was dry and hoarse.

"Lady, the sun is hot within the heavens and I have a camel's thirst! Will you bring me water that I may drink?"

She looked at the bearded man in front of her, the dust of the journey caked upon his sandals and a strange light burning in his deep-set eyes.

"Surely, good sir, straight from the well, if you will follow."

And as she turned he added, "And a bit of bread to eat?"

She stopped at that and looked back at him with a troubled face,

"Alas," she replied, "I would gladly bring you bread and meat besides, but we are without, ourselves. Everything that was left us, when my husband died, has gone. Now there is nothing left, only sufficient oil and meal for one last bake and then my little son and I must starve. Forgive me, water I can gladly give, but you must look elsewhere for any food."

The stranger's shoulders went back. He seemed to tower over her.

"Bake your meal, woman," he commanded. "But bring me first of your bread and, by the Almighty One, the God of Israel, thy oil shall not fail, neither shall thy meal run out from this day forward until that same Lord God of Israel shall gather again the rainclouds upon the country of His chosen people!"

How confident he sounded! How triumphant! She knelt before him.

"Oh sir, have mercy on an honest widow. My home is poor and meagre, but my roof would be honoured to give you shelter. And at my table you shall be served before my son…!"

He strode after her, commanding and erect, and the door of the house of the widow of Zarephath shut behind them on this first miracle of God through Elijah the prophet from Tishbe in the hills of Gilead. For, true to his promise, the oil of the widow did indeed stay full in her jar and the meal never entirely emptied as day succeeded day and Elijah awaited the summons of the Almighty in the little town of Zarephath.

But the voice of God stayed silent and, little by little, the voice of his hostess penetrated his conscious mind instead.

Slowly he became aware of the hard world in which she lived and the ends to which she had been put to keep her household sheltered and fed.

"I am not a good woman you see, my lord. But the baby was only small, he never knew when I stole out at night. What was there left to sell then but myself? And men pay well.

They were all strangers. Not our own folk, you understand."

Her pitiful pride touched him. He, the ascetic prophet, glimpsed another world, another code of values, where sin and shame glowed in a softer light than at the Courts of Baal and Jezebel.

He sat in the doorway later, turning the matter over in his mind. The little boy waddled over to him on fat, baby legs and plonked his bottom down on the step beside him in the sun. They sat as silent companions, man and child.

The boy's wondering eyes fixed themselves solemnly on the absorbed face of the prophet. Then he broke into gurgles of delight.

"Look. A fly, caught in your beard, Great One. He's come to live with you! Look, there's a fly…" He bounced with his excitement.

Elijah instinctively put out his leathery hand to catch the little one as he tumbled sideways. As he did, a further, startling truth flooded across his mind: just so did the mighty God hold out His arms to catch His beloved children, those simple, ordinary folk who tumbled, tottered and fell in their ignorance and in their weakness, just as this innocent baby at his side.

In Samaria he had been overwhelmed by the mightiness of the battle, at the clash of powers of greatness, the Lord the God of Israel against the sovereigns of Samaria! Now he glimpsed another, deeper struggle.

Well might he, Elijah, proclaim the wrath of God and hoist the banner of the Lord before the panoply of Jezebel. Better for him to mind that the spoils they wrestled to possess were these, the souls and bodies of the common folk, the widows, shepherds, farmers, all who toiled to win an honest livelihood, the aged ones who dozed the day away under their olive tree, the young ones who played around their feet fashioning their castles in the dust with baby fingers...

Little people all, but it was in *their* cause that the great God called him, Elijah, to the fight. So that no longer might they be betrayed and trapped into the clutches of the ravenous Baal like helpless children gone astray and lost.

He pondered on, and as the days went by, the widow sensed his deepening understanding.

They fell to talking quietly together on the roof-top when the shadows of the palm trees lengthened beyond the city walls and the cool of evening breezes brought relief from the daytime heat. Together they would wonder at the escape of Elijah from King Ahab's court and the daily miracle of the great, black ravens by the brook in Gilead.

"Tell me again about your God," she would plead like a traveller thirsting for a drink.

And he would build the Tower of Babel before her eyes again and then scatter the proud ones in their many tongued confusion.

Moses came, leading the unruly children of bondage as a patient shepherd herds his flock.

Joseph the town-dweller in Egypt, too. This one she had a greater understanding of, among all the busy commercialism of Zarephath.

But the sacrifice of Isaac by his father Abraham she could not bear to hear twice over, too close did it seem to her own small son lying asleep beneath them on his pallet.

"Not the little one! How could your Almighty be so cruel? Is He another Baal to snatch a baby from a father's arms?"

"Not so," explained Elijah. "You do not understand. This was how he showed our father Abraham that never again should human sacrifice be offered on His altars. The angel stayed his hand to tell him this for all time."

"But to tear a father's heart in such a way! And he a friend, or so you said, of the great God!"

"But how otherwise should He discover Abraham's trust in Him? A trust above love of husband, wife or child? Above wealth, possessions, power or rank?"

But she was not to be persuaded. "Your God is as jealous as the Baal himself if He begrudges these."

"It was so special. Abraham, you see, was to be the father of us all. Not just the father of Isaac or just the head of an important tribe. His children were to be the children of the Lord, set apart from all others, dedicated to the worship of the One True God."

"But now they worship Baal in Israel, not your One True God. Surely your God should slay them then, or burn them with His fiery breath as Baal does?"

Elijah's eyes were sad.

"His fiery breath even now does indeed burn the land beneath their feet. The grasses wither and the waters fail. But this is but the chiding of a loving father, not a vengeful God. I see now, He only waits for their repentance and their understanding. Your Jezebel has snared them in the net of Baal and they are weak and frightened.

I understand it so much better now. They are like helpless sheep, led astray from their good shepherd. God, I think, has chosen me to call them back to Him, but how it may be done I neither know nor hardly dare to think."

"Courage, good master," the widow put out her hand in sympathy. "If your Lord God can stoop to save one child, like Isaac, perhaps He can save the thousands also."

She sighed.

"But it is hard to understand a God so strange and great. Still, glad I am I was not Abraham. I could not have given my little one to Him for all the chosen people in the World, I love him so.

He has grown so thin of late and quiet and has a colour to his cheeks I like not. And in his sleep he cries out as his father did. Could your God help to better him, Elijah, if you asked Him, do you think?" she added wistfully.

Elijah nodded. "He shall be in my prayers tonight, I promise." He rose. "Now we must to bed or we shall be the cause of gossip in the house…"

He lay in his room off the outer staircase later that night musing upon his exile. He listened to the coughing of the little boy below him, in the house. In his mind he could see the anxious face of the widow bent over her child as her hands stroked his hot forehead.

"Lord, in Thy mercy, keep the boy from harm."

He fell asleep but, with the dawn, the frantic cries and sobbing of the household shook him brutally awake.

"He is dead! Dead! Our little one, our light, our only joy! Is there no pity in the gods? No mercy, prophet man? What is your God then? Is He a tyrant that He punishes me like this?"

On a shocked impulse Elijah stretched out his hands and snatched the child away.

Turning with him, he climbed back up the steps to his room. Almost savagely he kicked the door behind him on all the clamour and reproach that blocked out the very presence of God Himself.

The cries were suddenly cut off and the room was quiet, almost as a tomb, he thought grimly. His arms tightened around the still body. He groped desperately for words.

"O Lord God, if You are here and if there is any love, any compassion in You, hear my prayer now for this little one! You gave me life in the wilderness. Give life again to this little child, I beg You."

He instinctively set the boy on his own pallet and flung himself across him in agony, willing him to breathe again. His own breath came in urgent gasps:

"O Lord God, hear Thy servant… O Lord God, hear my prayer… O Lord, give life, give life…!"

Three times his prayer rose to the watching silence and three times his voice increased in certainty as his faith grew more intense until…

"Great God be praised! The Most High be for ever blessed!"

The still figure moved beneath him…

The thin chest rose against Elijah's rough tunic, up and down, up and down. For a moment Elijah dared not breathe himself and only the muscles of his bare arms quivered as he held himself suspended, motionless, above the boy.

Never had he known a moment such as this! The Lord his God had spoken! The boy lived! The blood pounding in his ears seemed like the soaring triumphs of a thousand choirs! How great was the Almighty One of Israel!

He knelt beside the child, his hands hovering over the tousled hair and fearfully stroking the face like fingers daring to gentle a fragment of rare porcelain.

At last he awoke to the world and struggled to his feet. Out of the door and into the sunlight and, step by step, silently, down the white staircase to the staring group below. Gently he stood the child down…

There was a moment of incredulous silence and then the widow flung herself at his feet, her arms around her living son.

Her joy, her tears, flooded out in torrents like a bursting dam.

"Indeed! You are a prophet of the greatest of all gods. All that you have told me of Him is truth above all truths! Your mighty One shall be forever blessed!"

Elijah's heart was full beyond all speaking. His God had shown Himself at last! Here, in the very courts of Baal, His power had triumphed! And not just for himself, in secret, but for these alien, unbelieving folk and he, Elijah, had seen it happen, touched it, felt it working underneath his hands!

This was the sign for which he had been waiting. The sign of the Lord's power upon earth and before all peoples!

He heard his voice then answering the widow, but his mind was full of light. His feet followed blindly the path out of the city, his ears deaf to the clamour at the gate. Down he tramped, unseeing, on and on until his eyes suddenly focussed on the sea stretching endlessly in front of him.

He fell on his knees on the wet sand and raised his arms wide to the heavens as if to catch the very glory of his God from out the sky.

The little waves played happily around his tattered cloak and the breezes laughed around his eyes. ...so did the Lord God bend lovingly over His gaunt and lonely son and, stooping, gently raised him to his feet, well pleased at this, His second miracle through Elijah the Tishbite and prophet of the Lord.

Chapter 4

MOUNT CARMEL

FIFTY MILES ALONG THE COAST to the south, the sails of the ships hung lifeless in the heat and, up the fertile valleys of Samaria, the earth stood hard as iron. On the hills beyond it was easy to mistake the bleached bones of a dead sheep for the familiar white outcrops of limestone, they were so thickly scattered; while, in the royal palace of King Ahab, the dogs endlessly licked the marble floors to cool their swollen tongues.

When Elijah had proclaimed the wrath of God those three long years ago before the astounded court, Ahab had been quite frightened at first, until the satisfying crash of spears, proclaiming the royal salute, had reassured him.

Queen Jezebel at his side, had silently narrowed her eyes and quietly dispatched a hundred of her swiftest horses to bring the prophet back, dead or alive, and planned deliberately his public torture as a living sacrifice to appease the affronted Baal.

But Elijah had vanished and, with him, their fears too faded as the months went by. The olives and grapes were heavy on the bough and none but a fool expected it to rain at the height of summer. As the cool of winter approached they had long ceased to give a thought to the unkempt fanatic who had disappeared so quickly and had, no doubt, long ago become a meal for a hungry wolf. The winter was a dry one but the wells were still flowing and the barns only half emptied…

The hill people suffered most in the summer that followed as they patiently shepherded their flocks weary miles in search of fodder.

By the following year every stream was but a ribbon of dry pebbles in the creases of the hills and the rivers of the plain were tracks of dried mud winding to a glassy sea.

Jezebel, her elegant face contorted, raged at her high priests in vain and stormed at everybody else around her. Even Ahab was secretly quite relieved when his chief steward came, one day, with a grave face.

"The horses, Sire. Your finest chariot steeds. They are dying of hunger and thirst!"

So he was glad of the excuse to slip away from the stifling town and ride out with Obadiah in a desperate search for pasture. Disastrous if his enemies to the north or east should hear of his plight, for an army without its chariots would be no match for an invader.

"Curses again on this Elijah and his God!"

Thus steadily Elijah, in his absence, gained a greater fear and respect as each parched day dawned and the curse of the God of Israel loomed more terrifying as the sun climbed endlessly up to its noonday furnace.

The mills of God ground on with still measured intent as at last over the northern border of dying Samaria slipped the Avenger of the Lord. Elijah had returned to do battle for the Almighty and the wayward children of His Promised Land!

Was this the same Elijah who had huddled beside the brook Cherith before the first ravens had come with bread for his body and courage for his soul? This confident victorious figure who wore his tattered cloak like the insignia of a mighty conqueror?

He felt his whole being charged with a glorious certainty and a tremendous vitality. He could hear the hills on every side echoing his name.

"Elijah is here! Elijah is come!"

He felt the vast, unseen hosts of the Lord above him and all around and he marched as Moses himself had marched to lead the Chosen People out of their bondage.

"For it is I, the Lord thy God who will go with thee..." Had not Moses, with his last breath, thus charged the succeeding Joshua? Moses too had known this triumphant power within. Perhaps it was he, himself, who even now led the angels of the Lord who went behind him and before?

Obadiah, cresting on his horse yet another unfriendly crag, gazed down into the valley below and saw the scarecrow figure striding along at such a pace that the dust of the path swirled up in billows all around him. Then Obadiah's voice rang like a trumpet heralding the beginning of a mighty battle.

"Elijah!"

He launched himself down the slope. Elijah held him with unafraid eyes as he found himself bending to the ground with all the honour he would have accorded to Queen Jezebel herself

"Yes, my friend. It is I, Elijah. Bear the news to the King and to his queen that I have come."

Obadiah shuddered. "Have mercy on me, my lord. Remember I at least helped to save many of the priests of God in the great purge. They are still safely lying-up there, in the caves, awaiting better times. You don't know how her Majesty treated the horsemen who returned without you when you disappeared before." He felt suddenly sick at the memory of the butchered bodies of what had been fine, loyal soldiers so short a time ago.

But Elijah's voice rose, commanding and invincible.

"You will not be harmed. Go, tell King Ahab that I will be with him before the sun shall set this day."

Partly the cold fear in Obadiah's heart melted away under the heat of Elijah's assurance. He turned and felt the eyes of the prophet on his back, following him steadily as he mounted the rocky hillside until he disappeared from view.

But Ahab, King of Israel, had a different welcome for his enemy. His mouth curled contemptuously at this tattered upstart.

"So, Curse of Israel, you have come back to us, I see!"

They stood like two fighters sizing up each other's strength. But the blast of Ahab's scorn fell harmlessly off the prophet's iron defence. Elijah's voice carried clearly back across the ground between,

"Not I, the scourge and plague of Israel, O King, but you and your accursed queen, for your wickedness in betraying the God of our fathers to the Baals of Sidon!"

Ahab felt, rather than heard, the shock that rippled through the ranks of his soldiers. He clutched furiously for more ammunition.

"Look around you, servant of the Evil One. See the agony of suffering your master's curse has brought."

That was better. Now he had the respect of his soldiers again. He pressed his advantage.

"See how the country dies under your scourge! See how the finest of our royal chariot steeds starve in their stalls so that we stand, helpless, against the Syrian host!

What sacrifice more does He want, your God? Tell me! Or, by the bones of Jacob, I will roast His own prophet on His altar before the sun is set!"

So Ahab roared and raged until Elijah's upraised staff commanded.

"Silence! A sacrifice there shall be indeed. Gather all your people, O King, to see for themselves the power of the God of Israel upon Mount Carmel's height. Order all the Prophets of the Baal there to present themselves. Bring also two bulls and the kindling for their burning.

Then you shall meet the One True God and kneel to worship Him and all your people with you, so that, perchance, the mercy of the Lord may fall again upon these His wayward children, as the rain and dew of heaven."

He spun his cloak around him and, as he did, the dust swirled up into the king's eyes and then, when it had settled, he was gone.

Through the night the crowds moved slowly towards Mount Carmel and Elijah, alone among the branching pines, caught the first notes of their solemn measured chanting. Nearer it came and louder until he could see, across the plain below him, the long line of torches snaking its way towards the hill.

He turned up the path, lifted by unseen hands as his feet took wings, and burst out onto the summit like a runner breasting the tape. He fell in worship on his face upon the springy turf. The short, dry scrub felt cool and real as his fingers dug into it. How he loved the feel of the earth and the smell of the turf in the morning.

He was a man inspired. "Dear God," he whispered, "what miracles of life You give us! Today Your glory shall be shown to all the world and every single soul shall know how great You are and how great is Your love to all Your people."

Above his head the gulls soared in from the sea as the sun came up over the trees and the sudden breeze of daybreak swept the hilltop into life.

Suddenly there were people everywhere, trampling and shouting, and the world was full of noise and colour and the smell of sweat. Hundreds upon hundreds came the swarthy priests of Baal, their long robes flaunting in the breeze. Then came the two dressed beasts for the sacrifice, carried high on the unwieldy stretchers.

Then, "Make way! Make way! Back, you scum!" And, with a lashing of whips and a churning of hooves, into the arena sprang the chariot steeds of Ahab, King of Israel, eager for the fray.

Around the high square altar the priests of Baal made busy commotion, arranging the kindling just so, with much argument and confusion. Their slaughtered bullock was lifted, with tedious ritual, upon the wood and they gathered themselves around the pile in a wide, deep circle. The chief priests raised their rich sleeves to the sky and a silence descended slowly upon the crowd. Down it came. Not an eyelid moved, not a breeze stirred as all Israel awaited, breathless, the miracle of the mighty Baal…

Afterwards Elijah remembered the irony of the loud snort from one of Ahab's chariot horses that had cracked the silence. He discovered that he too had been rooted to the spot, holding his breath in the greatness of the moment.

The priest's sleeves wavered and gradually dropped. An impressive prayer-chant began in the heart of the circle. It rippled, louder and louder, to the far reaches of the swaying crowd.

"Great God, Baal. Hear us! Hear us!"
"Send Thy fire! Show Thy mighty power!"
"Send fire, O Baal!"
"Hear us… send fire!"

On and on it sounded. Sometimes a loud shrieking pierced the air, knifelike and then again would come the long, deep, wailing drone.

"Send fire, O Baal! Send fire!"

As the sun rose higher up the sky, so the movements of the priests became more and more abandoned until, at times, the circle became a frenzied mass of writhing bodies.

They leapt, they stamped, they screamed and tore their robes until Elijah was quite overcome with the ridicule of the sight and shouted to them to "Cool off, or their sweat alone will put out the fire even if it does arrive!"

Their antics held him fascinated. He goaded them on with jeers and mocking cheers.

"Shout louder! Perhaps your god has not yet got up. He surely must have overslept this day... Louder! Louder! Maybe he is busy cooking up elsewhere... or doing something that we shouldn't mention!" He laughed uproariously at this until the tears rolled down his craggy cheeks and glistened in his beard. He hadn't enjoyed himself so much in years. Oh blessed be the Lord the God of Israel for the best day of a lifetime!

The burning noonday came and went and still they clamoured for the Baal, imploring, cajoling entreating...

Knives flashed and red blood stained bright on the white robes as the priests slashed and tore at themselves in frenzy.

In the heat of the afternoon, Elijah drew back from the crowd into the shade of the trees. For the first time he took his eyes off the circle of fanatics and looked around him. Rough country faces looked shyly up at him.

Simple faces, lined with hardship, reflected his own simple, dogged endurance.

As he sat among them, silent, he felt a warm compassion flow through him and flooding out over all who crouched beside him waiting. The assurance of the psalmist David welled into his mind and, with it, he blessed them wordlessly:

"He shall cover thee with His feathers.

And under His wings shalt thou trust…"
(Psalm 91)

Stubby hands thrust a goatskin of water into his lap, and in the touch of the rough leather, he felt the responding warmth and comfort of their friendship.

They sat on… watching… waiting…

The shadows were growing long when Elijah at last rose to his feet again and tossed his cloak around his shoulders. Thus "armed" he marched out on the still droning, slobbering priests. The crowd parted like the waters of the Red Sea to let him pass until he stood before the altar of the Baal. All Israel hung upon his words.

"Enough, you priests of Baal!" And turning, he commanded, "Come!"

As a shepherd leads his wandering flock to safety, he strode across the Mount to where the broken altar of the One True God waited in the red glow of the setting sun. At the altar he turned to face the men of Israel who had thrust forward on his heels eager to show their readiness to help.

"Come, we will build again the table of the Lord! Who will raise the stones with me?"

"Aye, master. Stand aside."

"We'll have them placed!"

"Here, Enoch, get your muscles under there and heave with me."

With heads down and veins swelling along their arms they shifted the scattered blocks one by one into position. Twelve, for the twelve tribes of Israel, to be built into a huge, square table.

Then the youngsters were sent scurrying into the trees to fetch out brushwood for the kindling.

"Mine the biggest!"

"Mine the driest!"

"Mine to go on top!" All hoping to be the one to finally crown the altar of Elijah's God.

His was the authority now.

"Enough! Now we must have a trench dug all around the altar. Dig it deep and wide, good men of Israel!"

Wooden spades and mattocks dipped and swung as the men settled to the familiar actions of their livelihood.

"Reckon that be a fine ditch, there, master." With a sly look towards the priests of Baal, "Make a tidy grave for some as I can think of!"

They stood back, leaning on their tools with heaving chests, looking to Elijah for his next command. They watched him step forward and reverently place the pieces of the offering on the wood pile with unhurried care.

It was the hour of the evening sacrifice.

Then he stood back and ordered barrel upon barrel of water from the Carmel spring to be poured over the carcase and the wood beneath it.

Three barrels—six barrels—nine—twelve!

The water cascaded like a deluge and ran dripping out of the kindling and down into the trench so that the altar glistened like some moated castle in the fading light.

The men were openly puzzled and chilled into a sudden, doubting silence. For the second time on that momentous day only the breath of God stirred upon the mountain. All eyes were on Elijah but Elijah's eyes were on his God.

He stood, his head thrown back and his sharp outline etched clear against the violet sky. Not a sound could be heard except for the drip, drip of the water off the altar beating the measures to eternity…

Then came the ringing supplication of the prophet: "Lord God of Abraham, of Isaac and of Jacob! Show Thyself this day that Thou art indeed Almighty God in Israel!

Send down Thy holy fire upon our sacrifice!

Let it be shown, O Lord, to all the world that Thou and Thou alone art power above all power, Creator, Majesty and Glory!

And I, Elijah am Thine humble Word and most unworthy servant."

He raised his arms as if to embrace the huge and trembling crowd within their compass,

"And hear me Lord, hear me that these too may know

Thou art their true and holy God,

That this day they may repent and turn their hearts to Thee once more...

O God of Israel, hear our prayer!

Forgive Thy lost and faithless people...

Hear our prayer, O God!"

The words rolled, echoing, into the darkness like the prelude to a mighty symphony.

As the last syllable died away the whole hilltop was suddenly drenched in brilliant, silver light. Swift as an arrow, shot from the bow of heaven, the fire of the Lord transfixed the sacred pile. Instantly it burst into a towering pyramid of scarlet flame, of orange and of gold! The crowd fell back terrified, arrested like a pack of wolves before the hunter's fire...

Then they rallied. "The fire of the Lord!" they cried, those men of Israel.

"The vengeance of the Fearful One..." wailed the priests of Jezebel and covered their faces in their cringing terror.

With a violent hiss of steam the ghostly banks of smoke billowed up as the fire rolled down to the water in the trench. How the wood crackled and the flames danced and leapt and flung their showers of golden sparks into the night above!

Elijah stood like a statue in the firelight as the tongues of colour flickered across his face. With his own eyes he was seeing the Glory of the Lord. His heart exulted as he watched the licking flames proclaim the power of his One True God. His body drank in the heat that surged from the altar and he felt himself swept up, along with the huge banks of smoke, into the very arms of heaven itself.

Nor were the multitude crowded upon the mountain the only ones to marvel on that night... Down in the plains the watchers, at their doors, saw the sudden flame shoot up out of the darkness and, for them, it was as if a new star had been born. A star of hope. A star to light a wandering people home.

From hill to hill across the length and breadth of Israel flamed the beacons with their message:

"The God of Elijah triumphs over Baal! Rejoice! The God of Israel is at hand!"

And in their villages and in their cities, in their fields and on their farms, the chosen people of the Lord turned, once again, to follow a second Moses out of bondage.

Back upon the mountain their king, Ahab, reared his impatient horses in salute before the triumph of the Almighty and led his people in obeisance to the God of Isaac and of Jacob. Then, like any badly frightened man recovering from a punishing blow, he bellowed all the louder to cover his confusion,

"Arrest those lying followers of the false God Baal! Those serpents of iniquity! Those blasphemers... those..."

His voice was drowned in a furious roar from the crowd as they sprang to do his bidding, unleashed from the chains of their own shame by his words.

"Kill them! Kill them!" they chanted. For these were savage times and death was as common a companion as torture and suffering.

Elijah himself seized the sacrificial knife and, with his own hands, drove it hard into the helpless body of the Chief Priest. As the man staggered to his knees, a bloody sacrifice himself, so the whole company of his white-robed followers fell like a field of corn beneath the reapers…

The silent figures lay as stricken ghosts, empty and dead. A last flame flickered on the smouldering pyre and then the velvet mercy of the night curtained this awful triumph of the Lord.

Chapter 5

JEZEBEL THE QUEEN

WHEN MORNING CAME only the prophet and one man who had stayed to serve him stood by the blackened stones.

But the awe of the Lord yet lingered and Elijah, still overcome, was down on his knees, his head bowed to the earth. He lifted his face and sniffed the air. He smelled the tang of the salt and his eyes gleamed in anticipation. "Go, my son. Look out over the Great Sea and bring me news."

The younger man ran across the plateau and stared down to the thin, white froth that edged the sand below. The smooth dark water stretched westwards to a clear-cut horizon and the grey light of dawn flowed back across the azure sky.

"Only the waves, master, rippling along the shore."

"Go again, my son. There is a wonder on the breeze! Go again and tell me what you see."

"Only the first fishing boats putting out to sea, master, under a silent sky."

Again… and yet again… seven times the feet sped while Elijah thirsted in impatience on his knees. Then on the seventh time the feet came pounding back in breathless haste.

"A cloud!

I saw a cloud no bigger than a hand but growing fast! A cloud, master, like a man's hand."

"Fool! That was no hand of man. That is the hand of God! Run swiftly to the king. Tell him there is no time to lose. His chariots must come to Jezreel in the hour or they will flounder belly-deep in mud!"

And as the clouds of the living God formed up in their battalions out at sea, a wind rushed like an outrider across the mountain top, furiously scattering the pyre of Baal that stood alone…

The sticks swirled up into the storm and the mournful carcase left went tumbling over and over until it lodged, ironically, in the sheltering channel around the altar of the God of Israel.

Under a thunderous sky Elijah flung up his arms in triumph and ran, like some black and gawky bird, right down the mountainside, his cloak flapping like huge wings around his flying feet.

The iron chariot of the king lurched heavily as he fought to keep the horses steady in the gale. Elijah shouted to him as he ran past, but his voice was caught up in the hurricane and lost in the tossing branches overhead, while around him all Israel, it seemed, was pounding wildly across the plain, swept like a cloud of autumn leaves before the storm.

Above them the thunder echoed and re-echoed in the surrounding hills. There was a sudden silence in the sky. An ominous hissing, as when a great wave gathers back along the sand to curl into renewed onslaught upon the beach and then... down it came! The blessed, blessed rain!

Pouring like a mighty waterfall from the heavens, torrent upon torrent, engulfing, swirling, flooding.

In rivers of cool water it washed the hills and valleys of Samaria, wiping away the dirt and wickedness of a generation of idolatry. Over the plains the rivers heaved awake again while, in the mountains, rivulets of the love of God caressed the barren slopes to life.

Never again should a strange god hold unchallenged sway over the country of the chosen people. The earth was clean once more beneath their feet and the menace of the Baal was vanquished for all time.

Later still, a dirty scarecrow of a man, heaving and panting against the stones of Jezreel, lifted his face to the cool rain while yet another miracle of the Lord coursed merrily down his tired and dusty cheeks.

The beacons had flashed their news across the length and breadth of Israel. One corner only stayed unlit, the throne room of Samaria where the Queen Jezebel sat in awful isolation.

In the Great Hall the feast of victory set out, was curled and stale upon the silver plates. The high-hearted preparations of the previous morning had melted into a puzzling languor in the sultry afternoon.

The fresh ring of orders and the scurrying of obedient feet had lapsed again into silence, a silence which had become almost ominous by the time the cool of evening fanned the palace back to life.

Every sound came magnified through the listening windows, the scream of swallows on the pool, the far off piping of a goat-herd leading home his flock.

Feet now pattered to obey like frightened animals and each face mirrored the unspoken whispers, "Where was the king and where the victorious following of the Baal?"

"Why had they not returned with cymbal and with song?"

"What had been happening on the Mount? Why the delay?"

They slid into the tunnel of the night. The queen summoned her eunuchs in a voice now edged with apprehension.

"Escort me to the Audience Chamber! Wait upon me there. We shall sit fittingly upon our throne to welcome home our triumphant lord and king! Light all the sconces! Throw open wide the doors."

She stirred and harried them with her tongue and took her place with intentional ceremony. There she had waited all through the stifling night, outwardly a flamboyant sphinx upon her throne while, within, anger and lurking fear throbbed in procession through her seething brain.

The torches spluttered and went out at the approach of morning and the room grew dark and cold as the thick black clouds spread across the land.

The palace dogs slunk whining from the distant thunder. The noise roused the queen's attention and she raised her head to listen... "Was that the wind or was it... Baal be praised... it was the rain!"

Pattering, falling, torrenting down at last!

"All honour to the legions of her priests! All honour to the conquering Baal! Moon and stars, where was the king and all the court? Surely now they should be coming?"

There was turmoil everywhere and the rich hangings on the walls billowed like huge sails in the wind.

At last there was a second roar like thunder up the hill and this time, with it, an explosion of barking and shouting and the jingling of harness and the snorting of the heavy chariot horses fighting for their breath.

The palace doors burst open and in marched the king flinging off his dripping cloak and sodden gauntlets as he came.

Jezebel met him eagerly, but started back in horror as he flung his news of the contest on Mount Carmel with equal abandon.

Elijah was triumphant after all and the God of Elijah was to be the God of Israel from now on!

"But do not fret, my love, such things are only for priests and the like. What matters most is that Elijah's God has brought us rain. Wonderful, soaking rain! So that my horses will grow fat again and the country will grow rich!"

"Your horses, indeed! What have you done with my prophets? Where are the priests of Baal?"

Ahab's eyes slid sideways as he wildly transferred his attention to the clamouring dogs,

"Your prophets? All slain! Yes… well… there was no stopping the people when Elijah's God had accepted his sacrifice. They had to have *something* to turn their vengeance on. You didn't want them turning it on me…!"

"Elijah!" She spat the name as though it stung her mouth. "Elijah! Always Elijah! That murderer… dog…"

She clutched at her throne and the room, for her, suddenly turned cold as ice. Her world spun round her as the realisation of her defeat penetrated deeper and yet deeper. Not *all* her priests? All that glorious retinue who had proudly brought her, Princess of Sidon, to be Queen of Israel?

The triumph of her entry flared again before her eyes. The splendid train that had swept into the country with her, singing, shouting and dancing and had so swiftly spread the power and dominance of Baal through every grove and hilltop.

"Elijah! Cursed be the God of Elijah!"

Was she, the chosen daughter of Baal, to bow before this contemptible, invisible nonentity they called their God? This god of shepherds and of goatherds and descendants of the sweaty slaves of Egypt?

Her long sharp nails, gripping her hands, drew blood. The red drops fell, one by one, onto the floor. She looked down, bringing her hands suddenly up in front of her face. The pent up strain of the terrible night of waiting burst through her self-command.

"Blood! I'll have his blood! The blood of Elijah, *that* shall wash these hands! Wash them and bathe them. Baal, hear me! Before the setting of tomorrow's sun we'll drink the life-blood of that traitor, burn him, crush him, tear him limb from limb!"

With madness in her eyes she turned upon a slave and in a tone of steel commanded:

"Bring me my scribe! Elijah shall know there is still a Queen in Israel to his cost!"

She lashed her attendants with her tongue, dismissing them, but quietly calling back one dark Phoenician slave. He bent his head to catch her urgent whisper:

"Ride hard for Jericho and Gilgal, Demonicha. Fetch me from there the novices of Baal with haste and secrecy and gather, on your way, three score new babes spewed from these swine. Aye, and their mothers too, if they should cling to you, with throats cut ready to appease, in sacrifice, the fearful anger of our Baal."

He seized her hand and kissed it and swiftly took his leave, his bloodied mouth bespeaking the awful nature of his mission.

Satisfied at last, Jezebel turned back to Ahab outwardly content to accept his version of the contest and Elijah's victory while, secretly, the poison of her wickedness sneaked out again among the hills of Israel.

Together they took their thrones...

But what of their mighty vanquisher all this time? What of the feared Elijah?

Did he too sit upon a throne in temple-splendour, dressed in the noble vestments of a priest?

There seemed to be so many priests around now that they had all emerged from hiding in the hills. There were plenty of eager worshippers, as well, to follow them again to every ancient shrine.

Was that Elijah leading the procession up to Bethel? Or was that he, exhorting the wide-eyed worshippers on Mount Carmel's summit?

Or was that the tongue-tied, lonely prophet of the Lord huddled in the dirt at Jezreel's gate?... As indeed it was! For there Elijah still sat, in the frightful isolation that only the great can know, and too utterly and crushingly weary to even brush away the endless flies that buzzed and mocked around him.

A vast emptiness had come upon him. He tried hard to pray, but his mind fumbled tiredly with the once familiar words and he sat helpless while they bobbed cruelly away down the idle river of his thoughts and sank from sight...

So empty! Surely his God could not have deserted him after all that had taken place? He had been so near! So close! Like his own cloak upon his shoulders, his own heart within him and now... it was as if the Angels of the Host had marched right over his body in their triumph and left him trampled, broken and forgotten, in a wasteland of despair.

Perhaps his work was over? Perhaps God had no further use for him on earth?

He saw himself again, as if in a dream, radiant and exultant upon Carmel. Had he done it right? Yes. He remembered now, God had sent His sign—that was what really mattered, and the rain had come and Israel was restored, forgiven... Oh God! Where had he gone wrong?

Thus his poor, tired mind tormented him, its fine sensitivity drained and his gaunt body utterly exhausted.

Dear Elijah! Scourging himself down through the valley of the shadow of death. That narrow, frightening way that all who seek to find themselves in God must tread in darkness and in loneliness. Had he but known it, his very fear and weakness now were to prove his strength. For had they not led him flying from the land, stumbling in terror the endless desert miles, he never would have reached his destiny and met, like Moses, face to face, the God that was himself within himself...

"Ho there! At the Gate, you there! Scum, hold fast the horses and treat them with respect or your life shall answer for it!"

Elijah raised his head and saw the lathered horses reined in impatiently, scattering a shower of mud.

"Where is the prophet, then?" He heard the leader's voice carry across the gateway.

"Speak up, you accursed spawn of Abraham. Where is he hid? In the Queen's name, we demand to know it!"

The Queen! He cringed back against the wall, covering his head. This was the blackness then that stifled him. Fear of the Queen. He knew it now. He knew too the message that the horsemen brought.

"I, Jezebel the Queen, say this to you, Elijah, murderer! May Baal smite me where I hold my state if I do not make you, before the sun shall set, as cold and lifeless as the legions of my priests...!"

He could see them now, every time he closed his eyes, a sea of white, limp figures, silent under the stars. He shivered and clutched his cloak tighter around him. His cloak! That was it! He would make himself invisible. If only God would help him as He had when, guided by Jehu, he had fled the court of Israel into Gilead.

He scarcely heard the clatter of the horses as they wheeled to gallop back to their Queen, but, seizing his staff, he was up and across the chattering gateway and out of sight among the fig trees so fast that all Jezreel swore, upon the bones of Jacob, that the magic of the Lord had swallowed him.

So it was that fear gave Elijah wings to flee, goat-footed, under the very nose of his enemy, but this time turning south.

South to the wilderness of Moses, south to the desert where the fugitives from Egypt, harried like him by royal vengeance, fled to the refuge of their living God. South to Sinai where the Voice had spoken out of the burning thicket. Sinai, the habitation of the Lord.

In his panic and in the confusion of his mind he scarcely understood himself why he turned south. He only knew he must. He travelled the length of Judah, hiding in caves by day and stumbling along the unfamiliar tracks by night until at last the palms and ancient wells of Beersheba came into his view.

Here, still furtive and wary, he mingled with the desert Arabs who thronged the oasis with their camel-trains and merchandise. The young servant of Mount Carmel had followed him thus far, faithful to his new-found hero, and Elijah had been grateful for his company. But now he knew he must go on without him and face the wilderness alone.

So he sent the man back.

"Go, my son, and God reward you for your service to me. Go back to Bethel, loveliest of all the shrines. Tell them that Elijah is safe beyond the vengeance of the Queen and searches for a treasure he had found and lost."

The lad hesitated, uncertain to leave him so alone and friendless.

"Be off, now, get along," Elijah's voice was harsh. How he ached for him to stay…

The servant turned regretfully and set off back towards the north. Elijah watched him go. As the distance stretched between them and the boy grew ever smaller on the path he felt again that hopeless emptiness within.

He turned, almost savagely, suddenly hating all the people around the well who had friends to laugh with and companions to their comfort. No one cared about him. He groaned aloud in his despair, turning it into an impromptu belch as a sunburnt face peered up at him, suddenly curious!

He might as well be dead!

But self-preservation is an instinct stronger even than despair and, before he had fully realised it, he was hurrying on alone along the road that led south, into the desert, his sandals flap-flapping on the dusty track and his shoulders hunched in urgency as though all the priests of Baal and Jezebel were snapping at his heels!

Chapter 6

THE STILL SMALL VOICE

THE DESERT WAS AN AWFUL PLACE. A wilderness of terrifying shapes. All through the burning days mirages, beckoning, made mock of him. By night the eerie winds soughed endlessly among the rocks and filled his sleep with nightmares of confusion.

Now fear marched hand in hand with loneliness. He deeply missed the company of the young servant he had grown accustomed to. No one now to coax him into the shade to rest. No one to find him food and water. All was emptiness.

The sun was merciless. It beat upon his head and on his thin, bowed shoulders. The rocks beneath absorbed the heat and hurled it back into his face. It scorched his skin and licked, like flames of fire, around his legs and feet, sucking him dry.

But still the fear of Jezebel hammered through his head and drove him on.

"Faster. Faster! Don't stop! On, Elijah. The horses of the Queen ride fast. Fly ere they reach Beersheba and take to scour the desert for you! Faster! Faster!"

Hounded by nights of terror, seared by the days of heat, he tramped on blindly, with every step becoming weaker.

"Oh, that I might die," he sobbed. "Let me die, great God. Kill me and give me rest. Only let me die!"

In agony of mind and body he stumbled on a stone, clutched at the air to save himself, and fell. Finished and crushed, the bitterness of his ignominious flight welled up within, drowning the last flicker of effort and of hope. He lay defeated.

In shame he pulled his cloak to cover his head. This was the end.

"Kill me, great God of Israel," he implored. "Kill me, I beg You. I am not worthy to be called Thy servant. Only give me death."

"Yes, give him death," echoed the desert. "Death to the faithless. Death to the weak. Lord of the Loneliness, let him die!"

But the God of Israel came with compassion to His son Elijah. The clamours of the desert died into a murmur. The splendour of the sun was veiled in mercy. Softly the breath of the Almighty brushed Elijah's cheek and, instead of death, gave him death's counterfeit, a healing, soundless sleep...

Hour upon hour, as the stars wheeled in their brilliant march across the sky, Elijah slept, a sodden heap of sweaty rags half-hidden in the sand.

When the sun burnt hot again upon his back, he roused enough to crawl into the shade of a juniper that hung across the path. In doing so, he knocked against a phial of water that the miracle of God had placed there waiting for him. With an effort he brought it to his mouth and drank and fell again into a dreamless sleep.

Hours later as the breeze of sunset ruffled his hair and tweaked his leather cloak, he stirred again and thought the Angel of the Lord had come to him and whispered: "Wake up, Elijah. Wake and drink and eat. For you have far to go to find your God of Abraham and Moses.

"Go to Mount Sinai… Sinai… Sinai…"

The name echoed and throbbed within. He sat up, looking eagerly around. This time he marvelled at the water waiting there beside him and found the wheaten cakes that kept it company.

With stiff fingers he grasped and ate and, as he ate, he felt his strength come surging back. He struggled to his feet and, as he did, the crushing load of weariness and fear rolled slowly from him and was gone.

His thoughts leapt backwards to his agony, his stumbling. Could he be dead? He looked down at his scratched legs and his dirty feet. No, he was still alive.

He stretched himself, throwing his head back, glorying in his new-found strength. Above, high in the blue, now he marked the vulture that had glided hopefully above him, unseen, ever since he had left Beersheba. He stood staring at it, marvelling again how close with death he had walked. The vulture wheeled and silently sailed back to find a likelier kill.

Elijah, satisfied, gathered up his staff and bent to take what still remained of food and water, stuffing the phial and cakes into his purse. He threw his cloak around him, standing poised like a hound that sniffs the scent... Then he was off, striding, this time, with reborn confidence and with intent along the desert track.

Down through the wadis, over the burning sand, forging into the hidden wilderness. But for Elijah now it seemed that the farther he penetrated into the loneliness, the more he became aware of countless echoes crowding in around him. Echoes of that huge, unruly multitude, the chosen children of the God of Israel, who had marched this dusty trail five hundred years before.

For him their wailing and their shouting still clamoured in the air. Miriam was there, leading her women in a psalm of glory. Their timbrels jingled as they danced and sang their praises.

A thousand hooves patterned the gravel, sheep and goats and donkeys burdened with each family's possessions.

For him too, always at their head came Moses, that great-hearted shepherd of the Lord, guiding his charges with his wisdom and his patience down the long ages of their wandering.

Mile after mile they walked beside him, south to the mountain where the God of Moses and their fathers had hailed their leader from the bush that burned but never was consumed.

On the last night the echoes of their excitement rose to almost deafen him.

"Moses, Moses, where is the God of Jacob?"

"Will he meet us, Moses, on His holy mountain?"

"Will His breath shrivel us? What of our children?"

"Shall we be as angels?"

Then he fancied he heard the answering of Moses.

"Peace, my children. Sleep now, for the darkness is upon you. The Lord upon His mountain give you His peace through this last night and, at the dawn, His face shall shine upon you. Peace, my children…"

The desert hushed. Elijah fell asleep.

When he awoke the air was empty and all around was silence in the gathering light.

He looked towards the east… and held his breath. For there stood Sinai, towering across his path, range upon range of granite mountain, black and majestic in the pale dawn.

"Sinai."

Elijah breathed the word with awe. His fingers trembled as he laced his sandals. Excitement mounted high within him as he faced the mountain and finally he plunged towards it with a hungry eagerness to be among the rocks.

He did not turn and so he never saw the kindly spirit of the watching Moses fading quietly behind him into the dreams of yesterday.

The giant crags closed in upon him as he forged into a valley. He became imprisoned in a strange, grey world, cut off and quite alone. Now began the climb.

He slid and stumbled over the rough scree slopes following the upward path. Pebbles loosened by his clumsy feet re-echoed like a rain of hailstones into the cavity of silence. Thorn trees caught at his cloak with spiny talons.

"Beware, Elijah," they croaked. "Beware the wrath of God, the Lord of Sinai. Take care. Beware."

But nothing could stop him. He shook them off and pressed on urgently. Fighting his way by thorn and crag, over the guardian foothills, at last he reached the inner core, the towering peak that they defended with such grey determination, the heart of Sinai and the fabled place that hid, from human eyes, the fastness of the Lord.

Full of wonder he stretched his hand to touch the shining rock face. Hot and alive it quivered beneath his palm.

Recollecting the first command of God to Moses on the mountain, he hurriedly bent to put aside his sandals. He was on holy ground!

Now the pathway, like a staircase in the mountain, compelled him on. He could not stay. His bare toes clinging round the pebbles and his stick tap-tapping on the granite, he gained the summit of the lowest slopes. Rounding the jagged elbow of this first ascent, he paused to stand, a lonely silhouette against the sky. Then he was gone. Lost in the dazzling sunlight.

Lost in another world. A shining, golden world.

Burning it was! As he climbed, the heat reflected off the rock smote him in waves. The sweat poured down his face, ran in his eyes and blurred his vision. He rubbed at his face with his cloak and stood for breath. Yet still the stairway pulled and tugged him on,

"Make haste, make haste. Those who seek the Lord must not delay!"

Stumbling and slipping by turns but, spider-like in looks as well as in determination, he struggled higher yet.

Salt drops ran down, blinding him again. He groped for purchase from the rocks beside him... suddenly found nothing there to hold and lost his footing, tumbled headfirst into a cave and lay there sprawling in its sudden, unbelievable darkness.

The relief and coolness of it! He almost drank it in, it felt so good. Exhaustion locked him, prostrate, to the ground. With enormous effort he crawled to the furthest touch of wall and there, heaving himself to sitting, he leant luxuriously back against the cold, hard stone.

He sighed and settled deeper, enfolded in the shelter and the silence. He would rest here... only for a moment... and yet another moment... just one more...

His eyelids drooped, his chin sagged... he drifted down into unconsciousness.

Upon his sunburnt chest the prophet's tangled beard now rose and fell in wonderful contentment and only his measured breathing marked the passing of the hours.

The shadows of the mountains spread black pools across the desert when Elijah stirred again. Recollecting himself, he scrambled to his feet and hurried to the entrance of the cave. How high it was! Now he could see his path winding below and, out beyond the hills, the endless sandy wilderness, gold in the evening sun.

The thorn trees looked so tiny and unreal down in the valley. "This is how small our world must look to the Almighty in His heaven," he mused, "And we men must seem to Him like midgets, swarming so busily and swelling with our silly, self-importance."

The notion made him smile but left him sad. If the Almighty One was so remote how should he ever find Him?

"Dear God, where are You!"

As if in answer to his voiceless prayer, he heard a far off sound. He raised his head, his ears pricked. Was it the whirr of feathers? His eyes looked to the sky instinctively but no, no black, imperious ravens swooped upon him.

But still the sound increased, now drumming like an army out across the plain. Swiftly his eyes ranged to the desert, swept to the far horizon. Terrifyingly there he saw, spread right across the land, a huge, grey wall of sand that rolled, like an ocean tidal wave, towards him!

Elijah was forced back into the refuge of the cave as the blast of sand and stones crashed down around him. Bushes were snatched from crevasses and smashed, like twigs, against the rocks! Long fingers of the wind snaked in to snatch at him, probing and sucking, then beating him into submission!

But the prophet was kneeling, radiant, in his cavern. His eyes were shining with anticipation. Here was his God at last! The Mighty One! Come in the conquering power of the wind! Reigning in the dominion of the storm!

His ears were deafened by the pounding fury and the swirling dust filled the cave with cloud upon cloud of choking darkness. But Elijah's soul mounted in adoration,

"Hail to the most high chariot of the Lord! Sped on the shafts of thunder! Born on the wings of the wind!"

But the pull suddenly slackened. The noise slowly subsided as the storm rolled over the mountain and out again into the farthest desert. The dust settled silently around him in the cave... and there was nothing left...

Slow tears ploughed down Elijah's cheeks. His shoulders bowed in disappointment. His God had not come after all. The storm was of the power of Creation, but the Lord he sought was not within its compass.

Dispirited, he got up off his knees. But there was little time for self-despair. Suddenly the ground beneath him heaved and shuddered like a thing alive! He was lifted up and thrown against the wall as by a giant hand!

In a nightmare he saw the rocks of the roof buckling and cracking above his head while, from the deep interior of the mountain, came the terrifying rumble of an earthquake!

Elijah was flung this way and that, tossed like the plaything of a maddened bull! For a moment he almost believed the Bull-God of the Sea-peoples had indeed materialised and was tossing the mountain on its fabled horns!

Could this be his God? This terrifying force that shook His holy hill in a paroxysm of fury at Elijah's trespass upon it? He found it very hard to think straight at all but, as best he could, he implored his God to strike him dead if this were so indeed!

But the world gradually righted itself instead and, to his relief, he felt the ground grow firm again under his feet. The thundering echoes rang less and less among the surrounding peaks until, at length, an even eerier silence flowed from the darkness into his lonely cave.

Elijah, bruised and beaten, staggered to the entrance and knew again that broken emptiness of spirit. No God had come in the brute power of the earth, of that he was very sure. Yet looking westwards to where the dying sun, still veiled in clouds of dust after the storm, sank to the world's edge, he found a lurking gladness in his heart that this was so. Could not his God be even greater than the solid strength of Earth and soar above the power of the Air?

"Earth," he murmured. "Air... and Fire?"

In a breath-taking and royal response to his hardly formed question, the setting sun suddenly burst out from behind the greyness and flooded peak after peak in a golden radiance!

In an instant the whole panorama was a blaze of fire. Each crag and rock, each flowing slope, glowed in a glorious sheet of burning light. Upstanding branches danced as trees of flame and through the hills, Elijah caught his breath in wonder, the desert lay, a sea of burnished copper, a tideless ocean of incandescent sand as far as his eye could see!

The whole world had caught fire around him. Even his own hands, as he stretched them out, turned gold before his eyes and the path up which he had climbed now flowed like molten flame down to a crimson sea.

His heart leapt as he remembered Moses trembling in awe before the burning bush. Surely his God was here! His God had come at last! But although he peered into the blinding radiance until his eyes ached, no longed-for voice commanded him from out of the holocaust. There was no message from his God...

Slowly the sun sank down below the horizon and the tide of gold ebbed into a far off stream of rainbow colours across the dying world... and then was gone. The chill of night stole over the downcast prophet.

He turned, suddenly very tired, and sat himself down dejectedly in the cave, back in the darkness. He sighed a great sigh and leant back against the rock. He closed his eyes and his arms lay at his side, nerveless and limp.

"Dear Lord," he whispered, "I have sought You here, at the uttermost reaches of my world. Where else now can I go? How can I live? Where can I hide myself?

Without Your strength I am helpless as a babe, as useless as an empty waterskin. Teach me only Your way, O Lord, for I am less than the lowest of all Your creatures, arid as the scorched dust of the desert waste, a futile nothingness without a God."

...And so Elijah finally came upon the simple, humble door which his beloved Moses had sought and found in his long exile as a prince of Egypt. The door so small that only those can enter in who set down on the threshold all they value most—their pride, the greed of their possessions, their desires, the illusion of their strength. The "eye of a needle"… the door to the Kingdom of Heaven!

He did not even know he had slipped through!

In the silence that came after, he felt weightless, relaxed, yet wonderfully complete. His breathing deepened and his gaunt body surrendered to the infinite.

In his mind he seemed to be moving through the back of the cave, following a wide tunnel into the darkness. Down, in truth, into the unknown depths of his own self.

There was no fear now in the darkness, only a wondrous sense of ease and freedom. He was free! Free of the shell of himself that the world had shaped. Free of its tangle of emotions. Free of its chains of selfhood. He moved towards a light and the light increased to fill all of the darkness, radiant with love beyond man's understanding. It poured around him in a flood of goodness and his soul filled, like a well, full and to brimming over, with that glorious warmth of spirit which is the loving of the Living God!

A deep peace entered in and from the core of stillness came at last the soundless voice Elijah recognised, at once, to be the voice of God Himself within himself. The Still, Small Voice of Truth.

The pages of his life opened before him. He saw them with new and startling clarity and sprang to accept the honest challenge of the Voice. Yes, it had always been his own, unconscious pride that had made his loneliness. Then, guided to an even more ruthless diagnosis by the inward voice, he understood how that same pride had stemmed, at root, from fear. Not, in this case from fear of Jezebel, but from fear of surrendering his own, fierce independence. Fear, again, of identifying himself with all those other teeming humans on the earth…

His eyes flickered wide open as the force of the revelation jolted him back to consciousness. His fingers felt for the smooth reality of his staff. It clattered against a stone. The beetle who had been earnestly investigating the possibilities of his cloak scuttled for safety.

"Don't be afraid, little one." Was that his voice or was it, he wondered, the voice of his new-found God, chiding one such as he for his own lack of trust?

How shamefully he had fled, beetle-like and fearful, when all the time the compassion of the Lord had followed him thus, longing only for his simple self-surrender. Now, reborn, renewed, he knew himself less even than the beetle, merely an empty shell and yet a shell so brimming with the love of God that he was part of everything that lived and everything was part of him, the sun, the moon, the stars, the earth, the rocks, the trees, the farmer at his plough, the widow at her loom…

"Oh Still, Small Voice," he cried, "Trumpet of the Living God, teach me Thy Way! Thine be the

Kingdom that shall reign on earth and Thine the glory in my little life!"

Silently came the answer to his prayer.

"Go, my son, back. Be as a shepherd to my sheep in Israel.

Teach them with courage, challenging their foes. Fear not the Baals of Jezebel. Armed only with the love of God, go back to fight for Israel and to win the victory!"

Elijah rose, took up his cloak and staff and faced his destiny.

"God of our fathers, stay within me all the way," he breathed. "O still, Small Voice dwell in my heart and let me hear Thy every whisper as my call to service."

Thus did Elijah, nearly three thousand years past, seek out the Eternal Truth and find the answer deep in his own heart.

Poised at the outgoing of the cave, he flung wide his arms and felt the joy surge through his exultant frame. Alone no more! Yet free! Thus surely had his fleeing fathers felt when they had watched the Red Sea sever them from the iron chains of Egypt! Free they were then and free he was now. Wonderfully, gloriously free!

He turned to peer back into the cavern darkness. So small the entrance that his spread arms gripped the rock on either side. Strange now, it seemed hollow and empty as the wells of Ahab in the drought. A dark and lonely nothingness!

He whirled his cloak and was away down the steep mountainside, perhaps enjoined in his heart, like Lot, to dare no backward glance. He strode the stony path with new spring in his step. Above him the stars sparkled like diamonds and a soft moon now clothed the mountain in a silver light. He felt at one with every rock he passed, with every thorny shrub, he knew them all…

The breath of dawn lay hushed upon the shadows when at last he came upon his waiting sandals. A time to rest beside them and he sank down heavily.

Suddenly the enormity of his experience struck him. He ducked his head onto his hunched-up knees, tightening his cloak around him as if to avoid the blow. Back in the world, and quite away from the holy atmosphere within the cave, this was the moment when his mortal mind must needs weigh up the revelation in the cold light of day.

This time of re-appraisal was to mark the moment of his turning, not only to the God of Power of Carmel, but against all the temptations of the world to the deeper, complete acceptance of the Still, Small Voice.

The spectre of his mortal enemy loomed suddenly before him, Jezebel the Queen, her talons curved to kill!

He drew his cloak yet tighter, gripped with fear.

We, who live three thousand years ahead in time and in the measure of God's power and mercy, should pause before we condemn Elijah for his sudden trembling. Jezebel's power was sovereign absolute! One word from her ruled death most horrible to any who opposed her will!

"Dear God, she is still there, throned in Samaria, lusting to tear Your servant limb from limb. Baal too still lurks upon the hills; his tentacles must yet be reaching out to draw his victims to their fearful end.

Am I to return to preach a God whose love is far beyond man's puny comprehension, to such as these? And can I challenge the lusting greed of Baal with only this sightless, soundless Voice of utter peace?"

He pondered deeper still, following the Voice again: "Yet are there not seven thousand of My faithful left in Israel?"

Indeed, had they not flocked in procession to every shrine when Carmel's fire had swept across the land? Could he instil the new image of the Lord into these faithful? Where Moses, prince and father, had never quite succeeded, could he, the gangling Elijah, yet hope to persuade? But all alone, humanly speaking, how should one man rally and lead so many and against so large a host and dreaded enemy?

He ranged the silent stones with unseeing eyes. Moses, he remembered of a sudden had laid, in like manner, his burden before his God when he too had found the task too great for one alone, and what had God commanded?

"That he bring all men of leadership before His face, there to be instilled with the spirit of the Lord himself."

Of course! This was his answer too. That he must seek a partner for his work, a man of his own kind, simple yet strong, near in his heart to God yet with a ploughman's wisdom in his eyes.

One name sprang to his mind immediately. Elisha! That was the man! Elisha, son of Japhet, raised like him in Gilead.

Now he knew exactly where he had to turn. Not northwards back along the way that he had come but east, across the wilderness to Edom and over Moab's heights to Abel-meholah in Gilead. Here he would find Elisha and then, with him as his companion and his help, he would continue west across the Jordan and so... to Israel!

The sun had risen from behind the jagged peaks during his musings and his valley now was filling, like a goblet, with its light. A breeze of morning flicked a papery thing against his foot. It glistened where it lay. He paused in taking up his sandals, mildly curious at its long, thin shape. A fragile, castoff snakeskin. It poised as light as thistle-down upon his palm. He was quick to read the farewell message of his unseen God. Yes, like the snake, his former skin was shed and gone, useless as this cast-off roll upon his hand and, like the serpent, new and shining bright, so must he slither forth into the world again and ever leave his old self empty, and forgotten quite, among the silent peaks of Sinai.

The cloak was swung, the sandals flipped and flapped their old, familiar rhythm and a grazing sheep high up upon the slope lifted its face, expressionless, to stare.

Jezebel would have echoed its farewell... Baa-aa-aa!

Moses, you will recall, had led his twelve tribes from the wilderness across the southern tip of the Jordan Valley to enter Canaan from the east.

Now Elijah was to slip, in his shadowy way, past Ezion Geber and through Edom and Moab and the Gilead, then crossing back into Israel.

Day upon golden day, night upon velvet night, the desert led him on. North by the Bear and east by the rising sun until the watching peaks of Sinai sank forever over the purple horizon and he became a tiny moving dot in a vast loneliness of ochre-coloured sand.

The bare hills rippled in the heat. The solitary tree, high in its rocky vice, stood motionless. No breath of wind, no sound. Only the gaunt black figure, dwarfed to a human speck, slowly crossing the huge amphitheatre of silence.

A watching hawk, still as a carved statue on its soaring perch, hooded its eyes in pitiless optimism. Soon the black speck would falter, gasping. Soon its spider arms would claw at empty air. Soon it would fall...

Its beak tilted imperceptibly. He caught the glint of sunlight on Elijah's upturned head. He glided noiselessly down upon the unseen currents of the heat to be at hand when the spirit faded and the body died.

But as he drifted nearer he heard the most unexpected sounds floating back from the upturned, tangled beard. Not at all the sort of sounds that came from a dying man.

"The earth is the Lord's.
And the fullness thereof..."

Line after line of the lovely psalm rang round the listening hills.

"Who is the King of Glory?
Lift up your heads... Ye everlasting doors!
The Lord of Hosts,
He is the King of Glory!"
(Psalm 139)

Elijah, far from being a dinner for the hawks and jackals, was very much alive. If his feet no longer danced the stony road, his heart did. It danced to the golden songs of David, the Beloved of the Lord. His God reigned within as a king upon his throne and the verses poured out his love and his wonder at the continuing miracle of His Presence.

"If I ascend up into Heaven, Thou art there.
If I make my bed in Hell, behold, Thou art there…
If I take the wings of the morning,
And dwell in the uttermost parts of the sea…
Even there shall Thy hand lead me,
And Thy right hand shall hold me!"

The rich phrases, passionate with meaning, soaked deep into the thirsty landscape. Surely they remain there still, the hidden treasure of the wilderness!

The country that Elijah was now approaching would have rung a crashing crescendo to his symphony of praise. This was the land of Edom, whose mountains, as if tossed, like Sinai, on the horns of the legendary Bull-god, now tumbled in undreamed of shapes and sculptures on either side of the deep chasm of Arabah.

This is the valley that plunges south as part of the Great Rift Valley that cuts clean across the petticoats of Asia Minor until it finally recoils at the forked tongue of the Red Sea in its eastern prong, the Gulf of Aqaba. At the point of recoil and in keeping with the entirely fantastic creation of the whole countryside, stands a commanding row of enormous statue-like rocks, known still as the Pillars of Solomon.

In spite of the inhospitality of the region, however, it was through here that the rich caravans on the King's Highway continually passed, heading north to

Damascus and beyond. Since the time of Solomon, merchant vessels had crowded the quayside at Ezion-Geber, laden with gold, ivory, spices and everything exotic for the kings of the Fertile Crescent.

Moreover, under the massive guard of the Pillars of Solomon at Timna, only a few miles inland, was the Deuteronomic "land whose stones are of iron and out of whose hills thou mayest dig brass." The copper mines of the Ancient World!

In Elijah's time, the smelting stretched right down to the port of Ezion-Geber. Here an even greater furnace was established among all the accompanying industrial development and along with the thriving quays and warehouses mirrored in the blue waters on the gulf.

Like any other port and cosmopolitan centre, it was an area alive with the sly trader, the cunning merchant and the rogue.

It was into this perilous crater of iniquity that Elijah was now making his unsuspecting way!

He was into the outskirts of it before he realised. His eye had been caught by the ominous layer of smoke that hung over the approaching hills, when the hand of his ever-watchful God (in the simple guise of a protruding tent peg) had tripped him up and landed him, face down, in the sand beneath his feet.

His long, long adventure into the world of Sinai had come to a final, if somewhat less than dignified, end.

"Your feet, my friend, would seek for rest before your spirit, it would seem?"

The kindly human voice settled like balm over Elijah's head, making him cool, yet of a sudden weak. He turned his face, still buried in the sand and saw a hand, low to the ground, outstretched in greeting. His own hands groped for purchase but his arms refused to take his weight and, as he raised his head, the world turned upside down and spun him down into a pool of black…

The proffered hand drew back and, with authority, summoned assistance, care and courtesy and then its Arab owner seated himself upon the cushions, beside the exhausted prophet, to watch over his long sleep with a delightful and untroubled dignity.

Three days and nights Elijah lay, fevered and babbling in the tent; then on the evening of the third, his acrobatic world righted itself at last.

How comfortable the sand felt! How like graceful curtains the rocks around him seem to hang!

He puzzled feebly at his whereabouts. Curtains only hung in shrines. Gilgal? Bethel? A portrait of an Arab hovered into view.

"And so, my brother, you return to us at last," the portrait said. "Greetings and welcome to my humble home! Your presence honours Haran, son of Shammar! Peace be to all your house."

"I…"

"Gently, gently, friend. You have already told us many things. Greetings, Elijah, son of Abraham!"

So it was that Elijah came to find shelter, friendship and great kindness in the caravan of Haran, the merchant from Damascus.

Under its powerful protection he travelled safely through the noise, the dirt and the dangers of the port and then up the great basalt and sandstone cliffs, high onto the plateau of Edom, jogging and plodding the dry and dusty miles of the King's Highway.

All day Elijah and his Arab protector followed the disdainful, measured tread of the camels. But at evening, when the carpets were unrolled and the black tents draped around them, he would be welcomed among the dark and glowing faces circling the fire-pit where the talk flowed long into the night, until the crackle of thorns had died to the whisper of embers inside the tent and only the rustling of camel-tethers broke the stillness of the night outside.

The camels fascinated Elijah. Perhaps he recognised a kindred feeling in their lordly disdain of the trifling and the mean. He grew to have a great respect for their patient acceptance of those huge burdens piled across each mountain back as day by day the procession re-assembled along the endless road.

After a time he came to appreciate their individual personalities. How different they were and how like humans! There were the bullies and the timid, the braggarts and the humble... the Ahabs and the Elijahs!

No Jezebel, however. In her place was a beautiful, gazelle-like beast, silky and strong, with hair so light that it shone almost white in the dazzling morning sun.

She was Haran's own especial darling. His beloved Rachel. His Rose of Sharon.

For him alone she would lower her proud neck in graceful elegance and rise to her feet, with all the majesty of a queen, to bear his house-load and all his richest possessions in stately sureness at his side.

Perhaps the hot sun encouraged Elijah's fantasy, but he came to see how Jezebel and she might have grown, like twins, from the same, royal seed. The one unfolding with fearless dignity and grace in the clear desert air. The other, equally strong at heart, but disastrously twisted and warped by the burden of her own jealous pride and poisoned to her very roots by the foulness of the Baal-worship of her native land.

And the heart of Elijah wept for the soul of Jezebel the Queen and with his tears, ebbed the last of his terror for her evil power. How could one tremble, except in deep compassion, before the face of one who scorned the Sun, and in her tragic folly, chose the path that was to lead her into endless night?

They crossed from Edom into Moab and the talk in the tent at evening swung naturally to the politics of Israel and of Syria. Travellers from the west had brought the latest news of Jahweh's continuing victory in Israel... but also of the untamed fury of the queen.

Haran ben Shammar's forehead creased into concern. "Tarry with us, Elijah, my friend. Surely in our country of Syria, you will be royally received and dwell in safety? Come with us to Damascus. A word in the ear of Hazael, the Chief Minister to the Court, and surely you will find all the support you need to enter Israel with an army at your back. Then you may topple King Ahab in his ivory tower and stamp the rule of Baal for ever in the dust!"

As a jealous neighbour of wealthy Israel, Syria was an ever-present enemy to the House of Omri.

Elijah was much drawn to the plan. It tempted him greatly. He had found an immensely satisfying kinship with these men of the desert. He loved them for their unaffectedness and their generosity. Their simple needs equalled his own exactly. Their sagging tents, under the brilliant stars, had given him all the friendship he could ever ask.

Travel with them to Damascus! He could have willingly travelled with them for ever!

The beards wagged on. The voices became even more persuasive.

"And Hazael is a close one... strong too..."

"The King himself puts great trust in him."

"Too much perhaps..."

Elijah suddenly remembered Samuel. Samuel the kingmaker of Saul and David. Sent by the Lord himself to make and unmake sovereigns, to set up and demolish kingdoms...

They seemed to read his thoughts...

"Did not your greatest prophet-judge, Samuel, anoint the beloved of the gods, David the shepherd boy, to be king over the mighty Saul? Come and be a Samuel from Syria!"

"Yes, come to Damascus, dear friend. Hazael and Elijah! That was a powerful partnership indeed! Come with us."

At length the fire died down. The blankets were laid out. The black tents slept.

All except Elijah's brain. That refused to sleep. Where was his Still, Small Voice? Why could not he hear its clear direction when he needed it so much? Had he not been led, as by a miracle, to Haran's tent? Surely the Lord God must mean him to journey to Damascus and seek power there to conquer Israel? Was this his call to arms? His call to raise a valiant host to do brave battle for the Lord?

But what of his God of Peace?

In the end he snatched up his blanket, wrapping it around him like a cloak, and left the sleeping ones to seek for wisdom in the darkness of the night.

This way and that he tramped, wrestling with his thoughts. How logical it seemed. To journey onwards with his friends and raise the banner of the Lord at

Syria's Court. Then how they would flock, the Faithful left in Israel, joining their seven thousand valiant hearts to march in triumph on Samaria!

Was he not minded of the seven thousand ones at Sinai? And was not this the Voice within his heart that urged him thus?

His pacing faltered... such a Still, Small Voice! Could he hear it then through all his great, inward commotion?

He sat down, rather harder than he meant, and the stab of pain broke through the endless record of his brain.

For the first time since he had left the tent... he sat and listened.

He faced the west, where the gouged chasms tumble from the Moab hills down into Jordon. It was very still. The sound of sheep he noticed first. The distant bleat, answered across the sleeping plateau top. He strained his ears to catch a fainter sound, a sound of water running down and trickling far below in the dark greenness of the winding gorge. So long since he had heard the sound. Almost, he thought, since he had sat and trembled while the Cherith brook had gurgled at his feet and laughed at him...

"Cherith," he mused. "And Gilead... and Elisha!"

Then his answer swept upon him and he knew, for sure, his journey led no farther along this highway of the kings. The highway of his Heavenly King lay down the slopes before him, down to Elisha at Abel-meholah. Down through the Jabbok gorge to where the returning Jacob, tormented like himself through the long night of yesteryear, had wrestled with the God within himself and, with the dawn, triumphed to win the name of "Israel"!

His dreams of glorious banners, marching feet, drifted into the night. His way lay clear: the road to Abel-meholah and to Elisha and then—the road of quietness and peace. The gentle seeping of the power of God through into hungry hearts... and now, in his own heart, at last he heard the answering chime of truth and certainty.

A warm breath hovered on his crinkled cheek. A gentle muzzle brushed into his hand to comfort him.

Back at the entrance to the tent he turned and saw that graceful, silvery neck arched like the branching of a candlestick above the headspring of the Jabbok stream...

The Travels of Elijah II Jezreel to Bethel

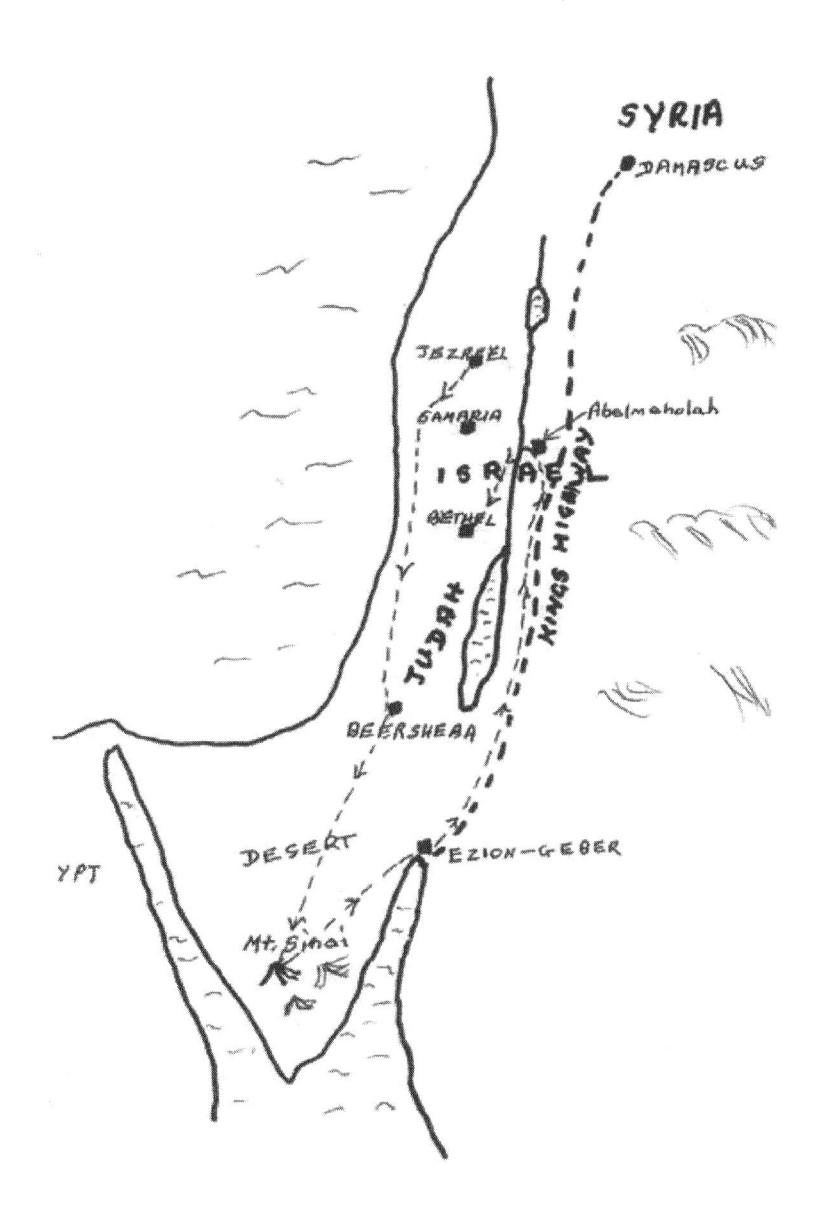

Chapter 7

ELISHA

FOR TWO MORE NIGHTS Elijah shared the warmth and comradeship of his companions. For two days more he trod the path at Rachel's side and then, in the hard morning light he stood alone, locked to the sand beneath his feet while the long camel train became black specks on the horizon and… was gone!

Mechanically he brushed his smarting eyes and felt the silky softness of his new cloak against his face. He heard again the quiet voice of Haran:

"Peace be to you, my friend. Peace be upon you all your days.

My tent will mourn your absence and my heart will keep you ever in its memory.

One thing I ask of you. One favour do I beg. Accept this camel cloak, a poor, unworthy gift, but maybe you can use it on your way…"

Into Elijah's arms he had thrust the finest cloth that he had ever seen. How rude and torn his old cloak looked beside it! Beautiful it was, a rare and lovely gift.

Then he had turned away and with his hand caressed his camel's neck.

"We will remember you, Elijah, brother of my heart, and one day, as your God is merciful, we three shall meet again…?"

His words still seemed to hang there in the air, half certainty, half question…

"We shall meet again…"

Well, his God was merciful, certain he was of that. Then they would meet again. He wished with all his heart it might be so…

Regretfully he turned at last and bent his steps along the slope and down… and down.

Then as he clambered from the scorching plateau into Gilead's hills, that newly comprehended, gracious God welcomed his home-returning prophet with a veritable festival of flowers, bedecking every ledge with stars of pink, carpets of blue and gold and, everywhere, green leaves, green branches and green buds flung at his feet in gay extravagance.

Sheep scattered from his path and goats, perched on the white rocks, gave him friendly stares. Just before sundown he had climbed so low that he had reached the spring of Yabi's stream as it began its last few miles of fall into the Jordan Valley. In its ice-cold water he sluiced the last traces, from his legs and feet, of the grey dust that marked the King's Highway.

Splashing to his heart's content at first he did not hear the reedy, piping sound. But when at last he lay full out upon the bank, refreshed and quiet, it came to him from just around the rocks, a shepherd piping to his wandering sheep, gathering them into safety for the night around his smouldering fire.

He followed the sound and took the piper by surprise.

"Greetings, my friend, and the blessing of the God of Abraham!"

The pipe poised as the dark eyes above it searched Elijah's face. Then rough fingers welcomed him to sit. "Are you an angel, stranger, appearing like a spirit out of nowhere?"

Elijah chuckled, "No, I'm flesh and blood like you and tired and hungry. Will you share my supper with me and, in return, allow me to share your fire and company until the morning comes?"

"That seems a fair exchange," the slow voice of the countryman agreed. "Dates and figs! Well, we shall have a feast for supper!"

He knelt and blew the fire and, from the ground, appraised his new companion again.

"You don't sound like a stranger. Are you from these parts?"

"Indeed I am. I'm a son of Tishbe, down there, five miles this side of Jordan."

"Tishbe!"

The shepherd scrambled to his feet. "Tishbe? Where the great Elijah lived? Tell me, do you know him? Have you met him? If only he were here!" Elbows on knees, he sat in sudden furious dejection.

"Why? Do you need him now?"

"Not me, not only me. It's everyone! You've been away, up in the desert perhaps. You haven't heard, I see. Elijah brought down all the fires of Heaven and burnt up all the filthy priests of Baal. He is the bravest man who ever lived, then suddenly he's disappeared and nobody knows where or why…"

His absent fingers stroked the nearest sheep.

"Israel is like a flock of sheep itself now, straying and lost, wanting their shepherd. If only he would come… You're from Tishbe, you say? You must know him, surely? Know his way of thinking too, maybe? Where could he have gone to after such a triumph, such a victory?"

"The victory, I think, was surely God's," his companion fenced.

"God's, Elijah's, it's all the same! Jezebel's priests were beaten on Mount Carmel and the God of Israel and the honest Law of Moses were restored in spite of all her plotting in that ivory wasp's nest in the hills." He spat and ground the spittle with his heel. "See here, whoever you are, if you're going down to Tishbe and he is hiding there, beg him to show himself. Tell him we go a-mourning 'because of the oppression of the enemy'. He'll understand. By the great God of Abraham, we need him now!

> "O send out Thy light and Thy truth,
> Let them lead me unto Thy holy hill, And to Thy tabernacle..."

His voice soared up into the night and the flames suddenly crackled up in unison.

> "...Then will I go unto the altar of God,
> Unto God..."

Elijah's voice joined his. How good it was to hear the familiar psalm again!

> "I shall yet praise Him
> Who is the health of my countenance
> And my God!"

The triumphant ending rang round them, echoing.

The shepherd picked up his pipe and, feeling the apertures gently with his fingers, he played a line of notes lovingly, softly. The song of David, the shepherd boy...

> "The Lord is my shepherd,
> I shall not want.
> He maketh me to lie down in green pastures.
> He leadeth me beside the still waters,
> He restoreth my soul..."
>   (Psalm 23)

Elijah pulled his new cloak tight around him. He was surprised to find his hands shaking with a new excitement.

Jezebel! The name no longer dug sharp prongs of fear into his stomach. A she-wolf she would always be, but he was called back to shepherd Israel "in the presence of her enemies". Yes, he must lead them to the still waters in his own heart, the safe, sure anchorage of his new-found God.
"Then surely goodness and mercy shall follow me,
All the days of my life,
And I shall dwell in the House of the Lord for ever!"

By first light, with the stirrings of the sheep, he was on his feet and down the winding trail to Abel-meholah.

"Stay, stranger," cried the shepherd. "If they ask me, in the valley, who shall I say I met?"

Elijah wheeled like a falcon in full flight, his arms flung out,

"Tell them, Elijah has come back!"

"*Come back... come back...*" echoed the sunlit slopes. "*Elijah has come back*," chattered the stream.

"Elijah! Elijah! Wait!" shouted the shepherd.

But Elijah was already wheeling down again among the rocks, the silver of his cloak streaming out behind him as he disappeared.

Gilead the beautiful! Like a bridal path his way was still strewn, on either side; with a rainbow of wild flowers. Poppies, blood-red among the daisy flowers, wild pinks garlanding the rocks, anemones, a carpet on the slopes and white narcissus, all to welcome him!

Finally he came to Abel-meholah.

There he sought the house of Shaphat, the father of Elisha, and found it standing in the olive trees as it had stood long since when all his word had been "a bowl of summer fruit" and fishing, barefoot, in the stream and sleepy talk beneath the brilliant stars.

Almost he thought himself back in those far-off days when he caught the sound of whispering and laughing, like fledgling swallow chatter, from behind a barn. There he chanced upon three dark-eyed children clambering on and off a long-eared donkey, laughing and tumbling on demanding feet like puppies in the sun.

He stood and watched their antics, his bearded face creased with delight, until they saw him there and became, suddenly, three chubby statues with big, wondering eyes.

"Can you tell me? Is Elisha there within?"

The donkey shook his long ears slowly, thoughtfully and then, clearly considering the matter safely closed, turned off to snatch a quiet nibble down beside the wall.

"Where will he be, my little ones?"

After another long pause, one small arm raised itself and carefully pointed down the path. Elijah smiled his thanks. It was as he'd expected and, even as his shadow disappeared around the bend, he heard the twitterings starting up again.

Down through the olive grove in the gentle shade he walked, to where it swept at last in checkered flatness to the river's edge—the precious, fertile strip that took the plough. Here Elijah stopped and blessed the goodness of his God for earth and life and promise of the spring!

How good a scene it was! The fig trees sentinel across the fields, the broad, green bands of untilled soil, the patient teams turning the green to heavy, shining earth. And all encircled in a necklace, carefully strung, the familiar, low stone walls of Israel.

Up and down they went, the double-oxen, two to each strip, unconscious of Elijah watching them. Small wonder that he passed unseen for, like the chameleon that he was, he stood as gnarled and still as any olive tree, the greying of his beard matching the silver leaves exactly.

Team after team approached and turned and went. He counted them and knew that, of the twelve, the last would be Elisha!

As Elisha swung his oxen to the turn, heaving the ploughshare round, Elijah moved and, with his arms outstretched as if to greet him, flung his cloak over Elisha's back and quickly walked ahead to still the oxen and to hold the yoke.

He knew no words of his must sway Elisha's heart. His must be the choice and his, alone, the life-long sacrifice.

It seemed indeed, a moment out of time as he paced slowly on, following the furrow. He heard the oxen snorting, pulling on the shaft, but of Elisha—nothing.

Was he fingering the cloak and, shamefaced, summoning a score of arguments?

Was he gazing, heart-sick, over the lovely land, his inheritance?

Had he dropped his head to run for cover... consolation... courage...?

Imagination struck Elijah dead and cold.

Then suddenly, around his shoulders, came the kindly touch of rough hands and his cloak settled, like a benediction, back around his neck and a strong and steady voice caught him and held him:

"Elijah! Father!"

And Elijah felt the sun shine suddenly in double glory as the loving fetters of his God silently yoked him to Elisha for the remainder of his life on earth.

"Let me first give a feast to say goodbye to everyone, my parents and my friends. Then I will come with you, my father, willingly and with no delay."

The oxen were unyoked and freed for ever from their bondage. They followed the crowd of men, symbolic of the two chosen servants of the Lord, to be the sacrifice.

The plough was broken and the yoke and shaft piled high, in the customary manner, to make the fire. The feast was set. Elisha's farming days were over and all Israel now lay waiting for God's chosen ploughmen. Their furrow was to cut deep into the history of their country. Their harvest was to be the triumph of the Lord!

Chapter 8

ELIJAH RETURNS

NEWS OF THEIR COMING spread across the country like shafts of sunbeams dipping into hidden corners, suddenly filling all with light.

An excited whisper in the market-place, a murmur among the shepherds at the well, a whistling goatherd calling from the hill and the message sped to yet another of the "seven thousand of the faithful".

Jehu, making his early morning inspection at the city gates of Samaria, stopped casually beside a merchant unloading his burdened donkey.

"What news from the south, Ben Ahmed? Do you bring us any jewels from the desert in your load?"

"Aye, Captain, I do. The rarest one of all to feast your eye on. It has a masterly setting too, new-fashioned by Elisha from your own, good Gilead. You know something of his handiwork, I think?

But it was too precious to trust to the journeying here today. I left it safe in Gilgal for your honour's examination at your leisure."

Jehu slipped a token into his hand.

"Good, your wares interest me. Come to my quarters after the Audience and tell me more about this precious stone."

He continued on his way, checking the sentries and the defences thoughtfully before retracing his way back to the palace. So Elijah had returned! At last! His heart rejoiced, but warily. How long would it take the news to penetrate into the Queen's apartments and how would she seek to take her revenge this time? There was great danger here. While Jezebel lived she lived for vengeance. Only another miracle, surely, could save Elijah from her venom!

In the days that followed a quiet descended on the palace and the town. Night fell.

"All's well on the western wall!"

"All's well on the Gate." The cries of the night-watch floated out into the listening darkness.

Jehu, with the Captain of the Watch, leant over the hard stones of the parapet, peering out into the night. The lights of the scattered villages twinkled like nests of stars in the black hills.

Arieh, beside him, stirred, resettling the cross-strap of his sword and swore under his breath.

Jehu said softly, "Something afoot?"

"Nothing for us to meddle into, my Lord, if you'll pardon my bluntness. People who poke too far into the Queen's business have a habit of never being seen again. There's things go on at night, in that temple that I close my ears to, fast, when I get wind of them.

You'd best do the same, my lord, if you want to see sons and grandsons in your time!"

"Mm," Jehu still stared out into the night.

He turned on Arieh abruptly. "You take over here, Arieh, for the next watch."

"Now look here sir, don't run your head into the Queen's noose. Or let me come with you at least. Someone to guard your back… Might come in handy…"

"No!"

Then Jehu's voice relaxed. "You're a good friend, Arieh. One of the best. But I'll do better on my own.

Give me until the first cock crows and then, if I am not back, send a party to search the Temple of the Baal.

But never fear, I shall be back. Here, take these for me." He slipped away, leaving his heavy sword and leathers in Arieh's hands.

The Temple of the Baal lay to the rear of the palace, lurking in a dark grove of trees. Jehu approached it noiselessly, one hand outstretched to part the branches as he slipped through, the other tightly gripped around the handle of his dagger.

The music and the chanting now came clearer to him through the gateway. He gained the pillars and was inside the courtyard in one flash of movement and was flattened back against the wall, his every sense alert to razor-sharpness.

Across from him, the inner sanctuary stood behind its windowless wall. The music now came loudly and weird chinks of torchlight pinpointed the heavy curtaining that marked the entrance. Jehu, silent as a panther, left the refuge of the wall and stole towards it.

The courtyard was miraculously empty. He smiled grimly to himself. The Queen-serpent wanted no curious eyes and ears to witness her devil-worship—that was clear. Good, the God of Israel was putting her fears to excellent use, giving him just the safety that he needed.

He straightened up, matching his height against the doorpost and with a careful forefinger and thumb, gently pulled the damask curtaining a fraction to one side. He lowered his eye to peer upon the scene within.

Through the haze of incense, at the far end of the temple, he made out the hideous statue of the Baal looming above the horned altar, its eyes glowing and staring in the torchlight. Beside it, the huge breasts of Ashtaroth, goddess of fertility, greased with the oil of their anointing, oozed thick droplets from their scarlet nipples onto her swollen belly. Her eyes stared straight at him and through the smoke she appeared to be hideously and malevolently real!

Soft couches lined the walls on either side, but all the space between seemed, to the silent watcher, one heaving, seething mass of bodies. The priests, their white and gold robes flying and the women in their rainbow silks all wove a hypnotic pattern of coiling movement to the insidious thrumming of the lyres.

Jezebel, in their midst, sensuously alluring in clinging, silken gauze, swayed her fine body like a thing possessed. Her long hair, tossed and spinning as she threw herself in ecstasy, licked in black flames across her painted face.

The music thudded to a wilder beat. Jehu could feel it sucking him, against his will, into its madness. Suddenly a cymbal crashed!

Like puppet-figures every worshipper stilled to a statue. A horn wailed once… and then again. Then awful silence!

The high-priest moved towards the idols, flung up his arms before them, and Jehu caught the sharp gleam of the metal in his fingers as his arm descended over the altar stone.

The howl of terror from the living victim, bound and helpless, screamed to the leering gods for mercy. But they gave no mercy.

The knife carved into its kill and its blood flowed, red and warm, into the silver bowls.

The worshippers burst forward in a wave of frenzy to drink to the glory of the Baal.

"Hail to the god of Power! Through death to life!"

"Through death to victory!"

The beating heart was torn from the corpse and proffered to the Queen who snatched it savagely.

"Queen of the Stars! Mother of Consummation! With this heart give me Thy quenchless lust for life and power! Call up the spirits of the dead. Beget in me Thy royal fertility!"

She sank her teeth into the crimson lump, then, gloating, smeared the blood over her breasts, her arms, her thighs...

Jehu, cold with horror, retched. His hand was tight upon his dagger when strangely the music suddenly softened. He held back for an instant. Or perhaps not he, but the Angel of the Lord restrained him, saving him for an even greater vengeance in the years to come.

The fingers on the harps, now muted to a smooth, seductive beat. It curled around the worshippers, lulling their bodies into a sinuous motion. Goblets of drugged wine passed from hand to hand, from lip to lip. Lascivious roots of mandrake took their place as if by magic, were caressed and bitten into greedily for the erotic passion secreted in their flesh.

The music now inflamed desire. The dancers faced each other, each male fronting a woman, their bodies weaving closer, twisting, writhing.

The priests flung off their robes and, naked and exultant, cried,

"To Ashtaroth, Queen of Desire! See, our seed is rich and warm! Do honour to the Queen of Life!"

Surging and gesticulating, each man bore upon the twisting and posturing body of his mate, tearing off the light coverings, clawing into the soft limbs, handling and contorting until each couple fell, as one, onto the couches or rolled on the floor, kicking with passion.

Jehu, his senses reeling, dragged his eyes away and staggered back into the forecourt. The nightmare orgy pressed like an awful weight upon his shoulders. He stumbled, blindly, to the outer gate and leaned against it, still trying to shake from his mind the horror of the scene.

"Jezebel! Witch! Murderess! Whore and adulteress! Great God of Israel, You shall be avenged!

One day her blood shall flow, even as her victims, and the dogs shall savage out her heart and tear her body limb from limb! Baal and Ashtaroth shall be brought low and Israel shall be clean! I swear it, on my life!"

Leaves rustled in the thicket in the breeze of the approaching dawn. From somewhere in the city a first cock crowed. Jehu looked up. His mind cleared. He was himself again. Squaring his shoulders, he turned his steps across the palace courtyard, out of the gate, and down the road to Bethel and his meeting with Elijah.

It was as well that Elijah had listened to the prompting of his still small voice and returned to Israel through Gilead, for King Benhahad of Syria was not the man to fight for the glory of Elijah's One True God.

His court advisers eyed the fruitful vineyards of Israel greedily. A first armoured raid on King Ahab's territory had proved unsuccessful but now a further march of the Syrian hordes towards that Jordan valley, near Aphek, sent renewed defiance to Ahab and Jezebel on their "Ivory Throne".

Ahab and Jezebel! In spite of their defeat on Mount Carmel they still reigned supreme in Israel. The splendour of their "Ivory House" in Samaria had become a legend even in their own time. It blazed with all the riches and the colour of the East! Every wall and pillar and all the furnishings, everything, was pearled with ivory! Reliefs breathed leaping horses, bounding lions, each figure delicately chiselled from its ivory base. It was the splendid palace of a powerful dynasty!

Now the levies were called up, the army gathered and drilled. Finally the thunder of iron wheels rolled out through the gates of Samaria, down to the Jordan valley and across the river to face the forces of Benhadad.

♣

How different Elijah's life had been! Far from the endless turmoil of court life, the summer had passed, for him, as a season of such unexpected joy as he wandered over the face of Israel accompanied by the young Elisha.

While courtiers and generals vied for favour and power in Samaria, no great struggle or proclamation clouded the establishing of his leadership. No clang of arms, no pomp nor any miracles of re-administration and rule. Yet like the glow of dawn after night's darkness or the touch of spring on winter's frost, so his quiet presence seemed to still all arguments and the warmth of his inner faith to melt all fears.

Until, in nooks and crannies the length and breadth of Israel, the flowers of God sprang beautiful to see. Men and women living with renewed heart, with brighter vision and with the light of the Eternal in their eyes.

To Elijah then, in Bethel, came the Lord Jehu even as the last rays of the sun gilded the western hills. There was no mistaking the warmth of Elijah's welcome:

"Jehu, my friend and brother! What joy to see you! Come into the shade. Rest and refresh yourself. This is a great occasion!"

"I rejoice to see you too, Elijah, and Elisha. I bring you blessings and greetings from all the faithful ones in Samaria."

"Samaria!" Elijah led the way into the house. He held the bowl for him to wash and then, himself, knelt down with the cloth to dry his feet.

"Samaria," he repeated. "When you have eaten, you must tell me how the army fares against Benhadad. And what of Jezebel?"

The friends supped quietly together, sitting cross-legged around the dishes. When all of it was cleared, Elijah asked again,

"And what of Jezebel?"

Jehu stayed silent. Elijah looked up, half hopeful: "But perhaps she learns, our Queen? Perhaps the God of Israel has softened her heart at last?"

Jehu smote his hands together.

"Upon the bones of Jacob, I wish that it were so!" he exclaimed. "No, she is steeped in evil. Blood runs through her fingers like a fountain. Listen to me, but do not let a word of this pass further than these walls—no, than your ears, for even walls have ears these days.

Last night I saw the vilest scene that I have ever set my eyes on. I, Jehu, veteran of a score of battles, I tell you I have never seen a sight more foul. Come near and listen.

It was Ariziah put me on to it..." From beginning to end he recounted his night of horror. When his voice stopped the men sat silent, stricken with revulsion at his tale. Then Elisha cried:

"Almighty God, can You not smite this harlot where she stands?"

A sob from Elijah drew their attention to him. The prophet was sitting in great distress with tears rolling down his cheeks.

"Why, Elijah. What have I said? Are you in pain?"

"No, Elisha, do not blame yourself. I weep not for myself. My tears are for the Queen."

"For Jezebel? She does not need your tears!"

"Yes, Elisha, the Heavens themselves must weep for her, damned as she is and lost. How terrible her end will be…"

"You are too good for me, Elijah," put in Jehu. "If her end were in my hands, I'd put them round her throat this night and squeeze until her painted face had turned all purple, blotched and putrid and the stink of her last breath had left her filthy body."

"She has a fate more terrible than that awaiting her," Elijah answered quietly.

He stood up and threw his camel cloak characteristically around his shoulders. "Walk with me to the temple, Jehu. You can tell me how the army fares at Aphek as we go."

It was a night ablaze with stars. The moon splashed silver and shadow across their track as they climbed towards the shrine. At first they tramped in the quiet of companionship, then Jehu burst out:

"You know, Elijah, you are mightily changed. Not in your looks, mind you. You're still the same tough bag of bones and leather that you ever were. But time was when I felt a giant beside your trembling, yet now you have grown like a cedar tree upon the mountain, so strong and firm that I, mighty man of valour that I am, feel I crouch as a bird among your branches."

Elijah grunted. He stopped by a patch of moonlight, poking among the grasses with his stick. Finally he bent down and tugged out a green plant. He held it out for Jehu to see.

"Take this now, my son. A wild leek. You know how the shepherds dress it for their pot? They cut off the root so it comes clear and free and then they peel all the soiled skins off, one by one, until all the dirt is cast away and the flesh comes true and white for the eating.

That's how the Lord God dealt with me at Sinai. Severed my roots of selfishness and pride and then peeled off my failings one after another.

And the darkest of all the skins He tore away was 'fear'."

"Fear? Is that a sin?"

"Aye, fear. The greatest.

For fear the children of the Lord bow to the lusts of Ashtaroth and Baal. For fear, indeed, you, Jehu, hate the Queen. For hate is born only of fear and where there is no fear there is no hate.

Fear wrapped my being. Oh yes, I cast it off at Carmel and at Zarephath while the strong Spirit of the Lord inspired me with His courage. But afterwards it closed on me again as well you know and hounded me right to the Holy Mount and into His healing arms.

In God there is no fear and then no hate, no striving, man against his neighbour, and then no despair."

He tossed the leek away and laughed.

"But you are right, my good and honest friend, the flesh the Almighty left to cover my bones is as thin and scraggy as it ever was. Still, it does a useful service and is less to carry on my travels. Now you, Defender of Samaria, you must look the part! Tall and well set, thick muscles rippling down your arms. The Lord God needs fighters such as you.

But what of our fighters at the front? What of the army? Tell me, is the news good?"

"No, bad. None worse. Ahab sends brave bulletins, but we are outnumbered like a couple of kids facing a herd of rams, and every day Benhadad's priests march between the camps parading their idols and shouting: 'See the gods of the Plain! Look well on them before they tear you limb from limb! Do honour to the gods of Syria, children of Israel! Remember, here your own God has no power. He is only god in the hills. Here it is our gods who will win the battle.'

"Ahab stands firm and waits for their attack, but morale is slipping and I doubt he can hold out much longer. I wish…"

They had reached the temple and Elijah beckoned his friend inside. He seemed suddenly to have grown even taller.

"Wait for me here, good Jehu. I shall not be long."

He disappeared beneath the colonnade that ran around the outer courtyard walls.

Jehu was astonished. He stared at the place where Elijah had just vanished. Was it more urgent than the plight of Ahab then? Could he not have stayed to hear all that he had to tell? He marched over to the brass trough in the centre of the court. The water in it glinted in the moonlight and rippled when, frowning, he dipped his fingers in it idly.

He looked around. It was so quiet. Peaceful, rather. In front of him the sanctuary loomed serene and beautiful. There were lights within. He caught the glint of them as a slight breeze swung the curtain between the portals. Light within! Oh horror! That awful scene behind that other curtain! His eyes riveted on the doorway, almost afraid to know what lay within. He ascended the two steps to the curtain and light streamed across the courtyard and Jehu caught a glimpse of the white and gold interior delicately lit by branching candlesticks. Glory to God! It was a vision of such delicate beauty that he, the rough soldier, fell upon his knees. He knelt in awe.

Elijah's voice startled his reverence. "Thank you, dear friend, we need the prayers of such as you." He scrambled to his feet, abashed, but Elijah was already hurrying back towards the gate, explaining earnestly.

"We have no time to lose. All shall be well with Ahab, Jehu, if you have a man can ride at sunrise to the army on the plain."

"Why yes, Shemach, the second aide who came with me this evening; he has the best horse this side of Megiddo. What message shall he take?"

"Not message only, he must take the messenger as well! One of my prophets, Micaiah. Can it be done?"

"He shall be saddled and waiting. But choose a prophet who can keep his seat for Shemach rides as though Baal himself is at his tail!"

"Then," returned Elijah, smiling grimly, "with Baal at his back and the Lord Almighty at his head, God grant he'll be in time!"

Chapter 9

THE BATTLE OF APHEK
AND
NABOTH'S VINEYARD

THE PLAIN OF APHEK was a wide, flat valley sweeping from the plateau of Bashan due westwards to the Sea of (what is now) Galilee. Aphek the town, walled and solid, stood on rising ground at the head of the valley. Beneath it and spread to cover a mile stretch of the plain, were the tents and forces of Benhadad. Then came a wide no-man's-land west of which Ahab's army, almost impudent in its smallness, was drawn up in two wing formations lightly joined in the centre by the foot lancers.

For six days now they had sat watching each other, the huge Syrian bear and the twin dogs of Israel crouching for the spring. On the seventh morning, as usual, the taunting chants of Benhadad's priests carried across the lines to the tent of Ahab. The King strode out and greeted Obadiah abruptly:

"Benhadad trying to win his wars with words as usual!"

"And not doing too badly at it either, Sire, from what I hear."

The day wore on. The army roused from the noon break hot and restless. Here and there voices were raised in anger. Swords clanged between brothers. Hope was ebbing fast.

Then from the hill slope sounded the sentry's horn. Its long note wound, hauntingly, down the valley,

"Horseman approaching! Messenger from Israel!"

The camp was alert. Messenger? At this time? The posting from Samaria had come, as usual, at the morning Audience. Could this be the long-awaited, hoped-for, word from their God?

The galloping figure drew nearer in a cloud of dust. Now they could hear the hoof-beats… almost make out the rider. Rider? No, there were two! Two horsemen on one horse? And he who rode behind was all in white!

"It is the message from our God of Israel!"

"A prophet comes! Praise to the Lord of Hosts!"

"Way for the prophet! Way for the messenger of the Lord of Israel!"

Ahab welcomed him civilly enough:

"Greetings, holy prophet. You bring us a message from the Lord Elijah?"

"I bring you a message from the Lord, the God of Israel."

"Say on, holy one. We bow before the Lord of Hosts Most High. He honours us with the glory of His Countenance."

"Your lips speak fair, O King. May your heart echo what your lips proclaim."

"Assuredly, my good man." He added loftily, "You have our royal ear and full attention."

Micaiah deliberately turned so that he stood sideways to the royal chair and facing the many soldiers who had crowded in agog.

"Men of Israel, and yourself, O King! The Lord Most High has heard the wicked clamour of the Syrian priests. His wrath is kindled by their lying claims. Lord He is of the heights, but Lord of the valleys too. He rules the mountain and He rides the plain. In all the earth there is no God but Him!

Lord of the plain, He comes to lead you on to victory!"

The tent was jubilant. The soldiers flooded out to spread the news. "The God of Israel marches with us!"

"To arms!"

"Harness the chariots, the Lord has given us the day!"

Back in the royal tent the prophet stayed to give the King a final word of warning.

"The Syrians have maligned the name of the Most High. For this the Lord our God shall punish them with death. Beware, King Ahab, that you leave not one alive to see tomorrow's sun. This is the Lord's command, no mercy and no quarter, for thus saith the Law of Moses—

"Thou shalt not take the name of the Lord our God in vain.

The Lord will not hold him guiltless that taketh His name in vain."

Ahab listened impatiently. "Yes indeed, yes indeed," he interrupted when the prophet paused for breath. "My thanks to you and greetings to our good subject, the Lord Elijah."

He drew himself up proudly as the prophet inclined his head. "The army," he announced, "awaits its King! We march to victory!"

It was a glorious charge across the plain!

With superhuman force the horses of Israel thundered forward and carved their way into the hundred thousand of the foe. In the hideous confusion that followed the Israelites gave no quarter and the Syrians learned, to their terrible cost, that, hill or plain or valley, all is the footstool of the Lord of Hosts!

Of the ten thousand of the army of Benhadad only a contemptible handful now remained alive, one of which was the king himself! Not for him the hero's death upon the battlefield. At the first charge his cowardice had turned him out of danger and into the safety of the city of Aphek. Now he lurked, cowering with fright, in its inmost citadel. Hazael, his Minister-in-Chief, eyed his king dispassionately.

"We have lost the fight, my king, but now see how we will win the peace.

Leave it to me. We will play the beggar's part for you well enough to touch the King of Israel's heart, and tempt his greed, I'll warrant."

Clearly unarmed and dressed in humble sackcloth, the Syrian servants begged their way to the tent of King Ahab. Around their necks ropes dangled miserably to proclaim their absolute submission.

They crawled before the king and pleaded a piteous case... Their king was overcome. In torments of distress they bleated. Could he but make some reparation, some token of his everlasting gratitude to Ahab if he would spare his life? Anything! The king had only to name his price... The markets of Damascus were his for the asking and, with them, all the trading of the Fertile Crescent!...

Ahab was completely won across. The trading concessions were accepted with alacrity. The two sovereigns met to make their peace as Hazael had planned it. Benhadad returned to Damascus, beaten, but still alive enough to bear resentment for his defeat.

The army of the Israelites turned triumphantly for home... Then they came to the ford...and the prophet Micaiah!

Pointing an accusing finger at the king he demanded, "Where is the body of the King of Syria? Does it lie rotting on the plains of Aphek as the Lord your God ordained? And his servants? Did you not speak them fair, entreat with them and send them freely on their way?

Ahab, the Lord of Hosts decrees *your* life is forfeit for his life. Your peoples for his people. So shall it be!"

The king sprang up, his face a study of emotions.

"I die for Benhadad? I, son of Omri? Out of my sight, prophet, before I slice that head off from the misguided body that brought you here! Die, when I fight the battle of the Lord? When I lead His chosen ones to victory at His bidding?

Is there no justice in the heavens? No high regard for kingship?"

Angry and brooding now, he led his army back to Jezebel.

♣

For all the unwelcome prophetic utterances, the House of Omri had never stood more honoured and respected. Ahab and his queen were sovereign names to be conjured with through all the Ancient World.

With the markets of Damascus in their alliance, wealth poured into their country. Ahab plunged his hands into the growing mountain of silver in the treasury and purchased a forest of cedar wood from Tyre, unlimited iron for his chariots and the finest horse-flesh in the East.

Jezebel too indulged her every whim. Unguents and spices she ordered, precious jewels and silks to adorn herself—and incense for her priests!

With peace established on all his frontiers and such riches to his hand, Ahab returned to the activity which, after soldiering, he found most satisfying—building.

Building and monarchy had marched hand in hand for the chosen people ever since David, the Beloved of the Lord, had established his first palace on the newly captured Jebusite Mount of Zion, Jerusalem. Later, in the divided kingdom, King Omri had determined to found a splendid line and sealed his position by founding the new capital on the hill of Samaria and with sturdy additions to the strategic cities of Megiddo and Hazor.

But even these were as nothing compared to the superb achievements of his son Ahab. The huge blocks of stone, still in position in the walls of the ancient cities of Israel after twenty-seven centuries, bear solid witness to the incredible skill and precision of the royal masons of King Ahab.

But marble and ivory, though richly hung with tapestry and damask and wonderfully cool in summer, could be less comfortable in winter. Then, when cold sea winds blustered around the hill, the high state-rooms could become huge caverns of damp and icy draughts as rain lashed at the shuttered lattices.

Ahab was inspired. He would design another palace for himself and for his growing family—one in a favoured, sheltered spot where the winter months could be passed more agreeably for them all.

The location he settled on was adjoining the small town of Jezreel which itself nestles into the southern slopes of the Jezreel Valley. Westwards the valley broadened out to become the Vale of Esdraelon, the Armageddon of future prophecy, and down which Elijah had challenged the speed of Ahab's horses after the contest on Mount Carmel. To Jezreel they had come for safety from the flooding, for the hill of Jezreel lifts the town clear of the floodplain and above the deep, rich valley soil that lies in a fertile wedge between the hills of (later) Galilee in the north and the country of Samaria to the south.

The palace proved a delight. From its terraces the valley spread out like an emerald carpet, in the springtime its broad flatness neatly squared into cornfields, pasture and vineyards. Each precious unit was the possession of some ancient family and prized beyond all riches.

Ahab was well pleased both with the design and with the workmanship. As to the site? He pressed against the creamy limestone battlements to view the fine sweep of fruitfulness beneath.

Along the lazy curling of the river his good peoples' holdings spread from the hem of Mount Moreh, across the valley, right up to the foot of the palace wall. He smiled knowingly to himself; no wonder the wine of Jezreel was a rare one—these vineyards must be goldmines! He grunted. His treasury paid out enough in gold to buy their produce to make them so! The royal vineyards of Samaria yielded a most inferior wine...

Now he looked closer he could see how much more abundant *all* the produce was. The onions! At least three times the size of those his royal gardeners grew. And look at those fig trees! The leaves alone were twice the span of those that grew below the palace in Samaria.

He frowned. The view was not so pleasing to him now. Then his face cleared. Of course! How obvious it was! *He* must have a royal garden here, in Jezreel. A royal vineyard too. How strange he had not thought of it before! Too busy fighting to protect these people, too thoughtful for their well-being...

He turned back to the problem on his mind. A holding attached to the palace would be the most desirable. He craned enthusiastically to select the suitable, vacant plot.

But alas, the little fields of Jezreel lapped in waves of green, all carefully owned and tended, right to the bastion upon which he leaned. There was no vacant plot!

He thoughtfully studied his immediate neighbour's garden. Yes, that was exactly right. A flourishing vineyard too within its walls, he noted. That should yield royal wines from now on! He would buy this plot, pay the fellow a fair price for his holding and perhaps show the royal pleasure by an added favour—a contract to supply the palace kitchens or a silver dowry for his eldest daughter. How gratifying!

"Chamberlain, ho!"

He gave the man detailed instructions and happily watched him as he hurried down the path to Naboth's house.

He pictured the excitement that his visit would bring.

"The King! Our glorious defender and sovereign of the realm asks for my humble plot?

Most noble Majesty…"

Of course Naboth would be highly honoured to be the one to express the nation's gratitude. "Deign to accept my loyal gift, great king…!"

Benevolently he studied the fruitful view. The cottage could be made into a useful store… And those stone watchtowers, they'd come in handy too, their walls were good.

He straightened up and regretfully dragged his eyes away. It would be more becoming if he waited for the man Naboth in his throne room, a purse of gold set carelessly aside, more than enough to compensate…

So he sat waiting, the small ape on his lap busily munching at the grapes he fed her. Beside the throne two sleek, royal dogs blinked sleepily and curled down at his feet.

They waited…

The man was longer than he had expected. So slow, these country folk. Ah, footsteps at last!

"Yes, yes, have the chamberlain come in." He entered. Ahab's mouth opened to welcome his companion, to put him at his ease. But, what was this? There entered no companion!

No Naboth? What? No vineyard?

One look at Ahab's face and the chamberlain cast himself full length upon the floor. In fear and trembling he blurted out the surly Naboth's answer to his sovereign.

"His Gracious Majesty must know the Law of Moses. The holding is not mine to give or sell! It is the inheritance of my House. My father's father's fields. The Lord forbids that I should part with it, even to the King."

"The Lord forbid! What Lord? The Lord of Moses, Lord of ingrates, Lord of fools!" This was Elijah's doing! And those damned prophets, troublemakers all the lot of them. Stirring up the people to defy his dignity!

By all the powers of Baal, was he, the King of Israel, to stomach such an insult!

Curses on Elijah and on Naboth! Curses on the God of Moses and His stubborn laws!

Where were the gods of Jezebel? Where were the Baals?

They were the gods to crush this insolence!

His roars and curses shook the golden throne. The pet ape, terrified, leapt for the swinging curtains and huddled, chatter-frozen, on the rail.

In terror the palace hounds streaked for the doors with flattened ears and hid themselves beneath the couches, shivering.

The thick, black clouds of thunderous rage spread through the palace, choking out the sun, shattering the day.

Ahab stormed: "Bring me my carriage! Dolts! Fools! Standing there, gawping!

My fastest horses or I'll throw the pack of you to feed the hounds!"

The palace rang with bullying orders and echoing feet. At last, iron stamping in the courtyard brought the royal carriage. The king threw himself in, still raging and, wrapped in black fury, he headed for the hills and Jezebel.

The queen summoned all her wiles to try to restore his broken pride.

"To ride through heat such as this, my lord! Ho, dogs! A goblet to your sovereign's lips and scented water for his hands and feet!

Comfort and rest yourself, my love. Let not that scum of Jezreel bring you to such despair. You are too mindful of your people's good. Too fatherly towards the mannerless brood.

The land and all is yours. You are supreme. You do but lend these pocket-squares of dirt to your ungrateful subjects!

Cheer yourself and rest now in content. All will be well. This matter will resolve itself at your command..."

But all the velvet of his consort's tongue failed to cheer the devastated king. Her liquid voice flowed streams of sympathy, but he remained sullen and brooding and defeated.

At last she left him, lying on his couch, and retired to her own chamber to turn her agile brain to a scheme of sufficient deviousness and evil to satisfy her own, cruel pride. Now she had her chance! Now she would show the God of Moses and Elijah how a king should rule!

A sudden inspiration brought a thin smile of triumph to her lips. She would even convert their own dreary religious customs to her purpose!

"Bring the tablets here and light up the tapers to mark the seal of our royalty! Now scribe, write what I say:

"Elders of Jezreel.

We, your king, do herewith charge you to proclaim a religious fast. And therein do you take one, Naboth, of your city. Set him in high estate and then, before the face of all men, arraign him with high treason and with blasphemy!

Then we order you to take him straightway to the execution ground and have him stoned to death!

His lands and all his goods shall thereupon be forfeit to the realm. His line extinguished.

To this we set our seal and do command your instant serving of our royal will!'"

The scribe's hand shook as he wrote the awful doom of Naboth, but Jezebel watched him like a hawk, following the wording to the very letter, until the whole was finished, signed and sealed... and then dispatched!

Here, indeed, were echoes of royal David's infamy: "Put him in the forefront of the line. . ." But at least Uriah died a hero's death. In fact, given the choice, the one he would have welcomed most.

The murderer of Naboth needs must mark her victim with the brand of blasphemy and hell to have her way and cast his House and all his kinsmen from their land.

All for one square of Jezreel dust and a drop of royal indignity!

The air seemed stifling in the Council Chamber at Jezreel as the royal message was made known. Jonah, leader of the City Elders, replaced the parchment on the table with hands that trembled as the scribe's which wrote it. He examined the faces of his fellow-elders anxiously.

"Gentlemen, these are our King's commands."

"Our Queen's, more like!"

"Yes, Jacob ben Eli, the Queen's, no doubt," he agreed. "And all the more reason that we should attend to them." There was an uneasy silence in the room. Then one said meaningfully, "I see another colony of her priests has settled, like a flock of crows, at Endor. Scarce had they perched there than their fires lit up the skies…"

"There are others newly come to Dothan, too."

"And some on Tabor…"

"And south of Nazareth!"

The elders eyed each other furtively.

"The last man I knew who fell foul of the Queen disappeared one night… They say the priests commanded his attendance at their sacrifice when the moon was full." The speaker shuddered.

"After all, we have our sons to think of. And what is this Naboth to us? An ill-tempered, common fellow."

"A fool, too, to drag us into danger such as this." There was a mutter of approval.

A lean, sharp man spoke up from the far end of the table. "I think Jacob is right. It is our duty to obey the Queen's commands or we, ourselves, are guilty of rebellion and we all know well the penalty for that!" He fingered his neck expressively.

"The less we delay this matter, the better for everyone… even that fool Naboth. He must know the blow will fall sooner or later. The sooner it does, the better for him, and us, that's what I say."

His fist thumped down upon the table as he stood up, then, briskly,

"Now, Jonah, a vote on it, do you think?"

Jonah looked round unhappily, but found little encouragement on the faces of his fellow townsmen.

"Very well, a vote."

"Thank you, I'll count the ayes... Good."

He nodded to old Jonah. "No need to worry, Jonah, I'll make all the necessary arrangements and, after all, a fast is as good as a feast when it comes to trade." He patted him on the shoulder as they left the chamber.

"I know two rogues who would sell their own mothers for a piece of silver. We'll have them make a big showing of their accusation. Nothing murky that the Queen can forswear afterwards, you understand. We have our own necks to consider... and our standing in the town!"

God of Elijah, did you hear the cry of Naboth?

"I am innocent, my lords! I swear it!"

"You have sworn too often, neighbour Naboth, it seems," a hard voice cut him short.

In front of him, two villainous-looking men were loud in their condemnation: "We heard him say it all, we swear!"

Naboth looked wildly round for help but not one voice was raised in his defence.

"Have mercy on me! God of Abraham, hear me! I am innocent!

How should I blaspheme? How should I curse the King? I am a loyal subject to the House of Omri!

They lie who swear against me!"

Dirty, accusing fingers, sticky with bribery:

"There is the man! We do not lie!"

"By all the gods of Baal, we heard this man cursing the King and God!"

"No! I swear, upon the bones of *Jacob,* I am innocent!

Help me! Believe me!"

Father of All, did You not hear the cry…?

Yes, the Spirit of the Ever-living God, who misses not a feather dropped in flight, caught Naboth's cry and heard the murdering stones crushing his life away…

"Up, up, Elijah! Arm yourself afresh!

Search out King Ahab where he rides to preen himself among the stolen vines and slay him with My judgement!

The Curse of Baal consumes My Holy Land. Murder and lust and bloody sacrifice. Jezebel smears My people with her evil and Ahab licks the poison from her hands.

Rise up, Elijah! Girded with My Vengeance. Now thou shalt strike the House of Omri from the throne of Israel. Death and dishonour shall their portion be before the face of all My peoples. The fate of Naboth shall become their fate and all their children's children. Every branch I shall cut off and cast into the Fire!

Their cause is lost! Their sun is set! The Curse of God has come upon them and they shall see My face no more!"

Elijah then, the Vengeance of the Lord, arose and slipped across the hills to bring the awful sentence of his God to Ahab. Like a shade he passed unseen. Ahead of him, the King in greedy haste rode headlong to the doom his queen had brought upon him.

Before the Jezreel gates his horses shied at the smell of blood upon the stones. He whipped them on impatiently, scattering the dogs that licked and scavenged on the bones of Naboth.

How many, Lord, must die before the world is satisfied? Outside the Council Hall carriage and horses jangled to a halt as the city elders stood to give their greetings to the King. Ahab resigned himself, ungraciously, to listen to their speech. Poor Jonah faltered and fumbled so, over the formal welcome, that he earned himself a sharp stare from the King who turned to his companion in the carriage.

"What is the matter with the man, Obadiah? Is he ill? His face is ashen and look how his hands tremble around the parchment."

He swept his eyes suspiciously over the square. Obadiah followed his gaze. "There are a full score more, in the crowd, with the same, pale, hollow look, my lord."

"The gods grant a pestilence is not upon us. I've no mind to be kept here if it is. We have our royal safety to consider."

With a gesture he silenced the unhappy Jonah.

"Thank you, my man. We know your loyal heart without your words and we recall that lately you have earned our royal pleasure. You have done well."

He lifted his voice to include the silent crowd and repeated, loftily:

"You have all done well!"

The response from the crowd was bleak. Ahab drew back. "Enough," he snapped, "Drive for the palace. We have lingered here enough. This place feels ill to me, today; on to the palace, I say!"

Alighting in the palace yard, however, the refreshing beauty of the buildings restored King Ahab wonderfully. How cool it all looked and how clean! And now a garden to complete it to perfection. Magnificent!

He marched towards the walls. The valley lay below him, green and enticing. His eyes travelled across the fields, one by one, savouring the approach to his share of it, at last. Ah! There it was! His garden! The fig trees in their soldier rows, the herb plot spread along the path, the vines... All his! He breathed a sigh of royal satisfaction.

A distant wailing sounded a discordant note into his pleasant thoughts.

"Chamberlain," he demanded, "That noise? It offends our ear."

"Your Majesty, it is the family of Naboth, mourning their loss."

"Naboth! That traitor!" he scowled. "He had his just desserts. Quoting the Law of Moses at us, indeed, at us, his Sovereign Lord!"

Well, Jezebel had seen him for the traitor and blasphemer that he was. The dog! Let his corpse rot, but he'll not have that dirge spoiling his day!

"Have the family of Naboth moved at once out of the valley. By force, if necessary, and to our farthest borders. No, wait! Send them to the Queen... She will have use for them perhaps..."

That minor irritation neatly disposed of, he snatched the goblet held out by his servant to cool himself with the wine of murdered Naboth.

"Hah, wine of Jezreel," he smacked his lips. "A royal vintage, now!"

A wine and vineyard fitting for a king! It drew his eyes again and gave him a sudden, driving urge to stand within it. To plant his feet into the earth he coveted. To grasp it in his hands, feel it between his palms. All his! His earth to hold! His vineyard to possess! His triumph!

With as much haste as dignity allowed, he swept out from the court and descended by the newly-surfaced path. Arriving at the garden, his hand forbade any to follow him further. He, and he alone, should enter as a conqueror!

The sun was high, the sky was clear and hot. Sleek as a tiger savouring his kill, he paced the rows, deliciously possessing every one. Enclosed within the leafy walls, he never heard the muffled shouts that floated from the citizens of Jezreel! No whisper reached him as the waiting crowds drew back to watch the figure of Elijah carve his passage through… across the city square… and down the new path… up to the gate…

A coldness settled suddenly on the King, an icy chill around his neck! He raised his hands to pull his cloak the tighter and then… a fearful instinct wheeled him round to find the nightmare figure of Elijah watching him!

His courage turned to water in his bones.

"Elijah! Is it you, mine enemy?"

"King Ahab, it is I."

Between them lay the stillness of the dead.

The cloak slipped from King Ahab's nerveless fingers and covered the ground and, as it fell, so crumbled all his hopes, his dreams, his life…

If only Jezebel were here! He mouthed defiance but, instead, heard his words reshape themselves to helpless admission of his guilt.

"So you have found me out, mine enemy?"

"Not I, my king. It is the Lord our God who finds you out and judges you as… Guilty!

Guilty of the darkest crime that fouls the hands of man! Guilty of murder!

The blood of Naboth cries to God for vengeance. Hear now the dreaded judgement of His Mercy:

This time I bring you death, O King!

Death to yourself! Death to your Queen! Death to your House!

The Lord of Israel shall destroy your tree down to its smallest root. Nor shoot, nor branch of Ahab shall escape the knife of judgement. All shall be cut down because you have worked evil all your days and fouled the land with lust and treachery.

For this, last and hideous murder, your own pampered corpse shall lie, like Naboth's, on the stones as offal to the dogs. While Jezebel, daubed with her harlot's paint, shall spread her mangled body to be chewed and torn by scavengers before the palace gates!"

The prophet's voice rang loud across the vines. Ahab heard his sentence, cold with horror.

Defeat! Disgrace! After he had stood so high! And all his children, all the noble line of Omri! All his House!

"No! Mercy, Elijah! Mercy! I was tricked. I did not understand… Not all my line… My sons… Not all my noble House…" He babbled and flung himself, slobbering and clutching at Elijah's sandals, clawing at the straps... his legs... his camel cloak...

"Your life is over, Ahab. All is lost! For twenty years you have led Israel into sin and sacrilege. The Baals of Jezebel have mocked the Living God and snared his people into darkest evil.

The fate of Baasha and of Jeroboam is upon you. You must die!"

"Spare me, spare me, good Elijah! My sin was great. I see it now. Is there no hope for me? No pity at the Mercy Seat of God?

I swear, before the face of the Almighty, I do repent me of my infamies. I grovel to His throne. See, I tear my robe in anguish, cover my head with Naboth's dust.

Help me to plead my cause! Save me and be my teacher. Be my guide. As Heaven shall witness, I shall walk softly all my days, even as King David in his hour of sin. Remember Elijah, the Lord forgave the murder of Uriah!

I swear to sin no more and to restore all I have taken and much more besides."

His shoulders shook and tears of penitence flooded the mud that now lay caked upon his cheeks, matting his perfumed hair and clogging the tapering elegance of his beard.

Elijah stood still, looking now away across the valley, listening...

He turned to Ahab, grovelling at his feet, his royal robe in rags, his hands still clawing to heap more dust upon his head. Sternly he questioned:

"And what of Jezebel? Will she not snake her charms around you, as before, and snare you back into her wickedness?"

"No, on my life, I swear! I shall forsake her bed from this time forth. My couch shall be the boards of lonely sorrow and I shall lie in sackcloth through the nights to please only my God."

Elijah stood in silence yet again. A bird whistled one note of bird-song from a tree. King Ahab lifted his head, one saving ray of hope lighting his despair.

"Surely the Heavens have heard my brokenness," he breathed. "Say, good Elijah, may I live to magnify my Lord and serve Him yet, in meekness, all my days? I kiss the feet of Him whose wrath is terrible, whose sword of justice is the lightning thrust, whose voice is as the thunder in the storm."

"Enough," Elijah's voice was stern and curt. "Your prayers have risen to the Throne of Mercy, stained though they are with hideous, blackest evil. The Heart of the Eternal hears your prayers and searches your repentance.

Your crimes are great and for them all your House is forfeit. It shall be cut off. Others shall seize the throne. This sentence stands.

But as to you, O King. The Lord gives you your life, in mercy once again, to spend in sorrow in His service, as you have sworn. Further, as long as you live, the Lord shall stay His hand against your sons. Your eyes shall not behold the sunset of your line. Until *you* die you shall remain King of the House of Omri and of the chosen ones and be the humble servant of their Living God!"

Chapter 10

ELIJAH IN ISRAEL
AND
THE DEATH OF AHAB

THE HAND OF GOD lay upon the land of Israel and Ahab did indeed walk in the fear of the Almighty One for the three years that were left to him to live.

Peace reigned in Jezreel, in Samaria and throughout the land. Peace too in Judah and in Syria. Three golden years.

For Elijah they were three years of marvellous wonder and fulfilment as, with Elisha at his side, he travelled the winding valleys and the rolling hills of Israel. As a true shepherd he called his sheep by name and they flocked, in their thousands, to his trusted leading.

As he journeyed freely and at peace, his only herald was the tapping of his staff along the rocky path bringing him to the busy housewife kneading in her doorway.

She would glance up, impatient from exertion, to see whose shadow darkened on her step.

"Elijah! Lord!"

Then her hands would fling out in a rapturous greeting, showering a dusty welcome of fine flour all over the travellers.

"Why, Master..." her voice would hold abashed reproach, "That you should find me thus!"

Turning to lead them into the shade within, she would hiss aside, "Quick girl, up to your father on the hill and down to the stream to tell your brothers."

Word would fly round the valley faster than any swallow:

"Elijah has come. Make haste! Leave all and hurry back. The master honours us!"

Soon the little house would be a hubbub of black skirts swishing around the preparations for the feast, while the slippery ways down through the olive groves would echo to the clatter of hurrying feet.

Silent, the wide-eyed children would sit like eager mice amid the avalanche of activity, inching their way towards these momentous strangers to venture a nearer view. One, braver than the rest, might dare to steal a secret stroke of his skin cloak and then find himself suddenly sitting at Elijah's feet.

At this, like a little flock of sparrows, they would all take wing and settle round his knees and listen while he told them how he once had been as timid as themselves and run to the farthest corner of the earth in fear...

Then he would lead them to the rocky cave and conjure up the thunder and the fire, the earthquake and the storm. The children would huddle closer to the cloak, but Elijah would just smile, almost a smile of triumph, and his eyes would fill with gentleness.

"And there was the Lord Almighty all the time, closer indeed than you are to my feet, warmer and softer than my camel cloak, stronger than my stout staff… greater than all the world!" His voice would rise to a crescendo and then sink back into a whisper.

"And yet when He spoke, His voice was like a murmur on the breeze and I had to sit 'as quiet as a mouse', like you are now, to hear Him…" His words would tail off and the little ones would wait in breathless silence.

"A Still Small Voice. So near it seemed to come from right inside me and can you imagine what it told me?"

A sea of nodding heads protested at the question, their big eyes urging him to tell.

He took up his leather purse.

"Do you see this?"

The listening heads all bobbed in unison.

"Well," said the Voice, "that's just what you are like, Elijah. Just an empty, sagging, useless bag. But I, the Almighty, made you to be filled, Elijah! Filled with My strength, My truth, My courage.

Now you have seen for yourself your hollowness, now I can fill you full to overflowing with My life and with My love.

Go home to Israel. Tell them that I am their only One True God. To each a strength, a power, a life, a mother, father, friend. To each I am the dreams within his mind, the warmth within his heart, the strength inside his arm... the cloak across his back.

"Do you see this cloak?"

Their eyes lit up.

"I'll tell you how I had it given me, up on a road that stretched into the stars..."

And so the simple people of the hills listened to his teaching and took his Almighty God into their hearts. He shared their humble lives, their hardships and their joys and, quite unknowingly, built up a legend, brick upon quiet brick, of his own love and his own shepherding equal to that of his beloved Moses.

But meanwhile, back in the palace of Samaria, the two kingdoms of Judah and Israel, cemented at last by a royal marriage, had joined forces.

Ahab's spirits rose to the occasion and he was entertaining Jehoshaphat, King of Judah, right royally and, in the heart of all the feasting and the laughter, Jezebel the Queen!

But what a queen!

Jehu's drinking partner, a captain of Judah, filled up his goblet and swung it high.

"To the goddess of beauty, your queen!" he shouted. "A queen to rival Sheba. A masterpiece!"

"She looks well tonight," admitted Jehu.

"Well! You need more wine to clear your head, friend Jehu. She is magnificent!"

Jehu grunted in reply and added drily that Jehoshaphat at ease beside her seemed enslaved enough.

"Lucky man. I wish *I* had his luck," grumbled his partner.

"Luck! I'd sooner bed down beside a scorpion!"

"Ah, but she would be a scorpion worth a sting or two, I warrant. Look at those shoulders…" he smirked, "And those luscious lips… those eyes!"

Indeed, the sparkle in Jezebel's eyes that night rivalled the brilliants in her golden headdress as her brow dipped and rose in tending to her royal guest.

Her warm responses to his confidences charmed him mightily. Her wit, blended with such grace and sympathy, was captivating.

The taper lights were kind to her sharpening features, softening and rounding them. Skill of her art with henna and with salve had done the rest. Her eyes, carefully framed with shadow of fine powder, shone as dark pools of deep sincerity.

The King of Judah, wondering dreamily how to reconcile the infamous Jezebel of Baal with this fascinating and lovely creature, tried to steer their conversation into channels of religion.

She matched him at every turn. She drooped her inviting shoulders sorrowfully, let her long hands fall, helpless on the cloth. She was the much-maligned, the loving lady queen, whose every action was misunderstood and he, the truly generous and great-hearted king, became her devoted champion until his dying day.

The daughters of the royal house, too, were assiduous to entertain their guests.

The eldest, Athalia, handed in marriage to the heir to Judah several years since, was overjoyed to be among her sisters once again. "How like me she had grown," thought Jezebel with satisfaction. A second Princess of Sidon and faithful daughter of Astarte.

Over the shoulder of Jehoshaphat she watched her quietly rise, with her husband, Prince Jehoram, from the couches and lead him softly through the maze of servants towards the Queen's apartments and to her private shrine to Baal!

She turned an even more radiantly enchanting smile upon her royal guest. The feasting was but a prelude to battle and Ahab of Israel and Jehoshaphat of Judah united against their common enemy Benhadad of Syria.

By late spring all had been put in readiness. The banners were unfurled, the music swung. The armies of the kings moved down the hill to fight and die in Gilead…

On the eve of the battle, in his tent, did Ahab have a sudden premonition that his end was near? A sudden shiver of warning? He mused back on his last meeting with Benhadad.

"You remember, Obadiah, how he grovelled before us, whining for mercy?"

"The snivelling coward," laughed Obadiah. "How could I forget?"

"Exactly," said Ahab softly, "How could anyone forget? Benhadad most of all. He has a little mind. Perhaps," he sighed, "the prophet was right, I should have let him die that day. I did what seemed the royal thing…"

"You think he begrudges your generous treatment of him? Hates you because you spared his life?"

"Hates me enough to have me hunted down in battle before all others. I'm certain of it!"

And Ahab was right.

The King of Syria stormed at his battle-chiefs: "Fight neither with the great nor with the small, but bring me the King of Israel's head upon your shield and I will give a fortune to the bearer!"

"Then, Sire, he must not know you. You must wear the armour of a common soldier to disguise yourself."

"It seems a shameful way to fight but, if the King of Judah will agree, I think it is the only way we shall outwit him."

Jehoshaphat was fully in agreement.

"My brother, your life is worth a thousand fighting men. You are our champion. Nothing must be left to chance against that jackal of Damascus.

See, I will enter the battle under the royal banner so that all eyes shall turn on me. He bears me no ill-will so I risk nothing more than the usual hazard of the fray. On the other hand, you must be plainly clad like any captain in his chariot. Then may our God preserve us both to work His Will to victory and to many further years in His service."

In the grey light before the dawn the high plain of Ramoth seethed with subdued movement as the armies on each side drew into planned formations for the coming battle.

On the hillsides flanking the wide valley, the light foot soldiers scrambled into position, scattering the grazing sheep and goats to safety over the crest. The bowmen spat on their hands and tested the flexing of their bows. Skirting the lower slopes, fighters with sword and spear crouched ready among the hummocks, watching the sea of chariots jostling into line across the whole spread of the plain beneath.

As the first saffron tints of sunrise outlined the hilltops there was a further surge below as each fighter took his place behind his charioteer who held the reins for the excited horses.

King Ahab, in the armour of a captain, was well concealed. Jehoshaphat, in all his king's array, mounted to the loud hurrahs of the Judean troops.

Lastly, behind them, the strap hangers climbed onto the chariots and bound the thongs of leather around each wrist, secured to the chariot sides. Unarmed, these men protected the fighter's back with their own bodies as he leaned back to draw his massive bow and were a second pair of eyes to guide the chariot and give warning of attacking from the side.

Rank upon rank the horses pawed the ground. High on hillsides the winding of horn to horn signalled that all were ready. All stood upon the unfurling of the banners.

All the world, it seemed, caught its breath!

A silence… and then the kingly shout of Ahab:

"Forward! Forward, O men of Israel! Brothers of Judah, forward to victory!"

As two gigantic waves the chariot forces from each side reared up and swept across the ground between. Meeting, they crashed together and locked in merciless struggle under a choking billow of dust red as the blood that flowed from underneath.

The thunder of their collision reverberated, like an earthquake, and two huge flocks of birds rose from the shaken camps and wheeled into the sky. Shepherds across the farther ridges pointed in fear:

"See, already the first souls of the newly slain hover above the field. Death fills the air!"

They cried to their flocks and fled to the southern hills.

Hacking and spearing, the awful battle raged. The Captains of Syria flayed at their horses in their search for Ahab. The royal pennants of Jehoshaphat drew them to attack his chariot.

"The King of Israel!" they shouted. "Death to the Omri!"

Trampling the bodies of friend and foe alike, they spurred towards their kill

His strap-hanger was the first to see Jehoshaphat's danger. "A Judah!" he cried. "A Judah! The Lion! God save the Lion of Judah!"

The Syrian horseman checked, cursing and plunged back into the battle to seek the Chariot of Israel. Above their heads arrows were raining down as bowmen from chariot and on horse took aim and launched their deadly shafts. Spears hurled and bloodstained swords thudded into living bone and flesh or clanged against armour, sliced and shattered once again.

A sea of carnage, none giving quarter. Brave ones who died with courage in their hearts, cowards who found no time to be afraid and fell like horses, others who cursed the gods and fought like devils until they, too, slid to their knees, choked in a stream of blood.

In the thickest of the fray, King Ahab thrust and parried like the great fighter that he was and championed his countrymen with gallant words and action.

His brave attacking caught the eye of an officer of the Syrians, Naaman, who, sighting along his arrow, let fly in his direction. As fate would have it, Ahab had leant over at that very moment to snatch an arrow for his own bow from his sheath that hung outside his chariot. In bending, the plates of his armour slightly pulled apart. For one instant only he was vulnerable, and in that instant, the shaft of Naaman thudded home through the unprotected hairsbreadth deep into the body of the King.

He staggered against the charioteer and then pitched back.

"Sire, you are hit!"

"A chance arrow, nothing more.

Turn the Carriage out of the fight, good Dolan, I..." His bow dropped from his hands, "I... hold me... I must not be seen to fall! Turn the carriage... turn it...!"

But they were caught in the solid mass of the fighting. To turn the horses was impossible and every step plunged them yet deeper into the battlefield.

The King grew weaker. His body slumped as he desperately tried to hold himself erect.

"They must... not see me... fall," again he gasped. "Keep me upright... the King! I am... their king..."

Behind him his loyal strap-hanger, with a skilful twist of his wrist, shortened the leathers until he stood closed up against his dying sovereign.

"Lean your full weight against me, Sire. You shall not fall."

Thus, while the chariot rocked and swayed, like a wild thing, around him, his faithful servant kept him upright still, that none should guess his fate as, drop after drop, the blood drained from his body onto the carriage floor.

Hour after hour he stood erect and dying while the battle raged unabated and the sun climbed to its highest and then began its merciful descent into late afternoon. At last the blessed, failing light of evening brought the fighting to a close and both sides declared an exhausted state of truce.

None conquered. All had been spent in vain.

Then only did the lines relax and the desperate, royal charioteer manage to wheel his horses round and call for help.

One look from Obadiah was enough. His strong face paled with anguish.

"To Samaria," he ordered curtly, "And gallop for your life!"

A murderous fifty miles of jolting torture lay before the King. Down to the Jordan, over the valley and up... The rounded hills of Israel loomed like giant waves in a mighty ocean pounding in his ears!

And then, suddenly, it was gone, the agony and the thunder, and the life of Ahab, King of Israel, flickered, then went out. With a sigh, and that almost imperceptible, he was no more. His body at last slipped down into the carriage and lay quite still.

The King was dead.

The snorting horses pulled up the long haul to the Ivory palace.

"The King! The King! Open the gates!"

Across the courtyard came his radiant queen, elated by such speedy victory.

The chariot empty?

"Ahab?... Husband?... King…?"

But eyes that were glazed in death stared out of a marble face. Hands, cold as the grave, greeted his Jezebel!

He was buried by the palace he had loved, lying beside his father, King Omri, who he had tried so hard to emulate. The carriage, together with his armour, was taken out of harness and left in the palace-yard. Later it was wheeled into the wide, ornamental pool that provided washing and bathing both for the palace and the common folk.

Here, with much splashing and scraping, the congealed bloodstains were sluiced off into the water. In ever-widening circles of dull crimson it spread to the water's edge where the thirsty tongues of the palace hounds and city dogs lapped greedily at the life-blood of their former master and of Israel's king.

The curse of Naboth, the curse of the prophet Elijah, the curse of the God of Israel was fulfilled!

The Battle of Ramoth Gilead
- - - - Boundary of Israel

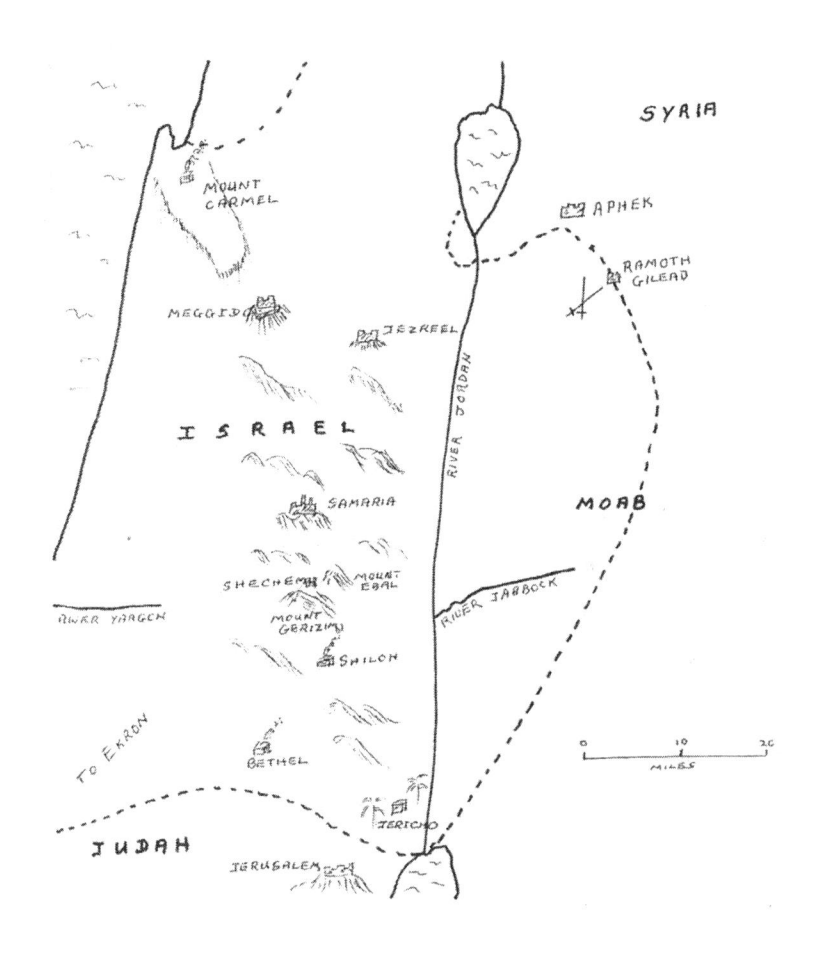

Chapter 11

KING AHAZIAH

FROM THE SWIRLING WATERS of the bloodied pool the cry rang out through Israel.

"Hear ye! Hear ye!

"The King is dead! Long live King Ahaziah, Son of Omri!"

Elijah, in the placid southern hills, heard the cry too and wondered why he wept to hear the news. A long and savage chapter of his life was closed. His "Trouble and his Torment" were no more and yet the tears welled in his eyes and trickled down his long, grey beard, so fine is the distinction between love and hate…

Suddenly he felt old and rather tired.

Taking Elisha's arm, he gathered up his staff and turned his steps towards the hallowed scene of his great duel with his dead enemy. Then when he stood again upon the crest of Carmel, he rested quiet, lost in the dreams of yesterday and there the loving whispers of the wind, in that High Place, brought comfort to his heart.

A fine shrine they had built there, on the famous spot! He looked round eagerly to place again the trees where he had sat among the people waiting on the prophets of the Baal. But his eyes swung out, instead, across the sweeping panorama of the Kishon valley flowing, in the luxuriance of spring, like a green river marching through the hills and up to Jezreel... and a vineyard... But that was now a story past and done. He turned deliberately and, with Elisha, walked towards the sea, his camel cloak ballooning out behind him in the western breeze.

Here was his place now. The path across the scrub was clear to the seaward ridge with no one but the passing swallows to watch the two friends walk right to the end and then dip out of sight.

Their disappearance was no miracle to the swallows. Their keen eyes would have marked the many caves in Carmel's western slopes as they wheeled and swooped among the lower wadis. Half hidden among the bushes and the trees were cave dwellings of ages remote even in Israel's time, spacious and sheltered.

It was to these that Elijah now withdrew, in Elisha's company, to pray, to rest, to dream long hours in peaceful shade and to commune in silence with that Still, Small Voice...

The cave, indeed, became a sort of point of pilgrimage and, to those who came, as they approached there seemed almost a magic in the air—as though the Angels of the Lord hovered unseen among the rocks and leaves, spreading a blessing all around.

Or was it near Elijah that the blessing centred? It was strange how light the cave shone round him and how a look from those wise, peaceful eyes seemed to pour goodness deep into their hearts. Those who came burdened low with troubles went away singing with a joy within, and those who came to bless returned themselves twice-blessed.

Food there was in plenty from the figs and wild locust trees, with water always bubbling from the spring and, for a bed, still the warm cloak of Haran gave him loving service.

Back in Samaria, the new sprig of Omri now occupied the Ivory Throne and kicked the palace dogs into submission—Ahaziah, the eldest son of King Ahab and Queen Jezebel. He sat now, impatiently awaiting the first petitioner at the Audience.

"Stinking curs," he scowled. "Let me have perfumes and the scents of spices in my presence. Am I not their King?"

His soft, fat fingers fondled the nearest maid-in-waiting.

"Now you, my dear, you please me mightily." He eyed her with a leer. "Do not withdraw, my dove. See, your King honours you."

His hands fumbled at her flesh while the Court stood watching silently.

The ring of sharp command along the passage came as a welcome interruption. Quick, decisive steps approached and stopped abruptly on the threshold. The curtains swung back.

"The Queen!"

Still she commanded their absolute attention and obedience. Still she stood upon her coming, the curve of pride upon her lips, her head held high!

She advanced towards the throne, inclining graciously.

"My royal King!"

Under her level gaze, her son's hands wavered, then dropped slowly to the lion arm-rests.

"Mother! We did not expect your presence with us at this early hour."

"No, my son?" Her voice was soft and purring. He welcomed her to her seat.

"But we are glad to have you at our side," he added hastily. "We trust the Baals looked kindly on us at the sacrifice?"

Jezebel took her place beside him.

"The offering was a rare one and most favourably received," she said with satisfaction.

"Good," he turned to his steward, "Now man, we are ready to give audience—but make short shrift of those who hang too long upon our patience. It is enough that we must smell their steaming odours! To listen to their tedious mumbling is an added burden. Quick man, quick. Who is the first?"

The chamber speedily filled with anxious faces and ingratiating tongues. The merchants and the craftsmen were led before the Queen. Closely she scrutinised all their wares, testing the damasks with her jewelled fingers, inspecting the beaten silver and the ivories.

The petitioners were guided to the King who met their cringing or their flattery with an unsmiling stare. It was a reception carefully calculated to cut short the voluble and to reduce the timid to hopeless dumbness.

The air became hot and thick with the smell of people. Ahaziah yawned and frowned...

"Enough," he growled. "Am I to be suffocated with the stench of dung and sweat? Steward, clear the chamber. The Audience is at an end!"

"The King is weary!" Jezebel's voice was as silky as the purple stuffs that streamed from the merchant's pack in front of her.

"Would you retire, my Lord, and rest yourself? The burden of State is ever tedious. Leave me to pass your royal judgement upon the petitioners that remain. It is a small weight that I shall most gladly take on your behalf. And do you rest, my son," she added coaxingly. "An hour upon the balcony will lift your spirits and refresh your noble nature."

Heaving his bulk out of the throne, King Ahaziah stood while the Court bowed low.

"You have our leave to hear our remaining subjects, good mother," he agreed ungraciously. "I shall withdraw to better company. Come girl, attend upon your King.

Burdens of State," he grunted. "It should be the business of the State to see the King enjoys his needful pleasures."

The balcony was high and cool, fanned by the breeze that wafted through the surrounding latticework. Ahaziah eased himself onto the cushions. His arm shot out! "Now you, my girl, you are my needful pleasure. Come and refresh your King!"

He fondled the arm he had caught. "Your skin is cool and scented." He pulled it roughly to his loose, wet lips. "See, a King pays it a royal homage. It is good enough to eat!" His teeth dug sharply into the flesh!

The girl cried out at the sudden pain and jerked herself free.

"What, do you deny your King? Ha, is the colt reluctant to be ridden? Must I bridle you to my seating? Here, bitch!" he demanded, and dragged himself up to blunder across the cushions, his arms outstretched to catch his prey.

The girl drew swiftly back across the balcony. The King, his foot caught up in the trailing stuffs upon the divans, fell heavily against the delicate tracery of the lattice wall.

"I'll have you yet and ride you a pretty course, my…"

The framework creaked beneath his weight, cracked, and suddenly broke. Ahaziah groped wildly, blindly, screamed in anger and then in fear as his heavy body toppled slowly through the shattered lattice and then dived headlong onto the paving far below!

Through the halls of Samaria re-echoed once again the curse of the God of Israel on the House of Omri!

They bore his broken body back into the palace. Tortured at every breath he took, Ahaziah turned for succour to the gods of his upbringing.

"Go with gold, and speedily," he gasped. "Ride to the mighty Baal-ze-bub of Ekron. He surely holds my life within his hands!

Beg him for mercy! Tell him that I, the King, kneel to him and him alone, for life!

Ride, you dog-heads and bring me the word of Baal that I shall live!"

All haste they made, the servants of the king, following the road down through the southern hills. Skirting Shechem, they turned west over the slopes and through the leafy wadis, racing for the coast plains and the Baal-ze-bub of Ekron.

But hard as they galloped, even faster sped the messenger of the Lord. Summoned again to work His will on Israel's royal line, ahead of them, Elijah sat beside the babbling waters of the Yarkon stream, quietly waiting in the shade of the oleanders and the waving palms.

Elisha, sensitive as always to his master's mood, had withdrawn into the trees to gather dates and figs and pomegranates for his later comfort.

To Elijah the charm and music of the running water filled his soul with unutterable peace. The tiny cascades, sparkling with life and tumbling with joy, personified the laughing, lovely spirit of his shining Lord. They ran through him, bubbling with gaiety, teasing the dust of age from his stiffening joints and tossing him back to that first stream in his life, the Cherith brook, that had spun the opening miracle of God into his growing understanding.

Then, tired after his journey through the endless miles of Sharon, he closed his eyes and listened dreamily to the chattering of the stream. There came again the memory of the stillness of a desert night when the distant clarion call of Jabbok's waterfall had summoned him back into the battle-ground.

And had his years of fighting really brought victory?

It was hard to believe it so, with the messengers of Ahaziah approaching nearer every minute.

Up and down the endless see-saw of the struggle had endured, with priests and shrines living and dying by turns as Baal and the Almighty strove, unyielding, for the soul of Israel. Would the battle never end? So many lives sacrificed! Restless as his stream, pressing and pounding through its rocky chasm, yet still the fight continued. How it dashed its way against the stones, Elijah thought! How like the Spirit of his God, challenging the strength of Baal!

Closely observing, it struck him suddenly that the greater the obstacles set into its course, the stronger became the power of the stream and the more beautiful became the swirls of water and the flying spray. Until, beyond the oleanders, where the rocks stood insuperable, heaved as they were in a wall against the flow, the river took a joyous leap into the air and flung itself triumphantly above them in a shower of even greater brilliance of rainbow crystals and of pounding foam.

At last he understood. So this is how it was! The greater stood the enemy, then the more vigour of the Spirit to defeat the foe. The darker the adversity, the brighter shone the glory of the Lord in overcoming!

Battle and struggle there must ever be as long as life endured, but no evil on the earth could hold in check the power of his God.

Here in the stream was writ the challenge of the Lord of Hosts, that in the darkest hours of the night the radiance of the day was ever born!

There came a furious thudding from beyond the shade, men's hasty shouting and the clatter of their arms. A lordly sweeping of the branches and the messengers of Ahaziah crowded into the wadi.

The leading horse was half across the stream when Elijah rose, like a giant satyr on the farther bank. The rider struggled to rein in his animal whose startled hooves splashed sparkling fountains in the dappled light.

Elijah's hand, upheld, commanded, "Peace!"

And then he spoke,

"Is there then not a God in Israel that you must shame the very soil you churn to bear the slimy grovelling of your king to Ekron's Infamy?

Go back, I say! Return and build a coffin for his carcase! The God of Israel is not to be mocked and thus he says:

The bed of Ahaziah shall become his bier and no more shall he sit upon a throne he thus dishonours with his blasphemy!"

Peering ahead in horror at these awful words, the rider's eyes took in the rugged outline of Elijah, his leather girding, the uncompromising sit of camel cloak upon his shoulders, the long, grey hair that straggled to his waist. Then he met his eyes!

Never had he confronted such authority and such assured command.

His knuckles tightened on the reins and, on a soldier's instinct to obey, he wheeled his horse full circle in the water and led his men, in silence, back along the path and out into the hills. Here, kicking their flanks in fear, they galloped straight back to Samaria and their dying king.

"A monster, gracious majesty!"

"With the dread curse of God upon his lips."

"He threatened death to your Royal Person from the God of Israel!"

Prostrate, their sweating foreheads greased the palace floor... though possibly they felt a *dying* sovereign not so much to fear... The groaning figure on the couch soon gave them reason to feel otherwise.

"Dolts! Cowards! Traitors!

Is this the way you serve the House of Omri?

What was this monster then? Quick, or I'll have your yellow tongues torn from your lying mouths! The King is not yet dead that you can spurn his orders thus.

Speak! Or you die!"

"Pardon great Majesty! Pardon and mercy! He was a hairy man, girt only in rough leather..."

"Baal give me strength!" The couch heaved with the fury of the tortured king. "Elijah, Curse of my father!"

In a foam of blood Ahaziah choked upon the name and in the rush of servants to attend to him the messengers made good their disappearance.

In his pain, Ahaziah's half-crazed brain fastened on Elijah as the cause of all his torment.

"Summon my finest company of guards..." He fought again for breath... "Before I die, I'll see that Tishbite torn to pieces by the very dogs that licked my father's blood. By all the Baals of Ekron, this I swear!"

Terror and mad desire fought across his face in horrible contortions, and as the clatter of the ordered horsemen faded down the hill, he sank back into his pillows to savour the savage sweetness of his black revenge.

Would the great God of Israel save His prophet once again? Or would He lead him to a martyr's death, now that his work was done?

No! The Almighty Alchemist, gathering the gobs of Ahaziah's hate into His everlasting arms, transmuted them, in an immortal breath, into a golden sunset for His champion!

High up on Carmel's rock He stood, unseen, beside the figure of Elijah, to watch the horsemen gathering to their kill. Their captain strutted forward.

"Man of God," he mocked, "Come down. We have you trapped on every side. Now pit your scrawny wits against the King, who summons you to die!"

Above their heads Elijah stared in silence out to sea and noted how the thunderous clouds, black as a raven's wing, were spreading from the west... covering the summer sky...

"If I be a servant of the Living God, may His power convict you where you stand!"

His shout had scarcely echoed round the hill, when the divine and awful wrath of Heaven descended on the fifty boastful men and slew them, where they stood, with lightning and with fire...

Livid with fury, the King attacked again! These too were slain with fire.

Chastened, the captain of a third approach humbled his knee at Elijah's citadel.

"Mercy, my Lord! Greatest Elijah, spare our fearful lives. Send not the lightning of the Lord upon my company, but only come with us, with graciousness and honour, to bring the message of your God unto our sovereign King."

Splendid as any pageant then, the slow procession of Elijah's glory wound its way along the paths of Israel. Shepherd and priest, peasant and prince, crowded to fling their reverence at his feet. Some ran before with palms to grace the way, others ran to fan cool air until Elijah's long, grey hair danced in the breeze they made.

Singing and garlanded, the cavalcade arrived at Megiddo. Here the great gates swung open and chariot and horse, the pride of Ahab's cavalry, came thundering down the slope to add their royal allegiance to the line.

Elijah called a halt. He stood above the multitude, a scarecrow figure raising up his staff for silence.

Then, as his voice lifted itself to sing again the psalm of praise of David, his face took on a look of incredible beauty and his ageing body, a radiant, kingly stance.

"Bless the Lord, O my soul.
And all that is within me bless His Holy Name..."
(Psalm 109)

The first, few notes hung clear and lonely on the air and then every throat throughout the valley took up the rolling chant. Like the roar of an ocean, so the deep chorus swept around the hills...

"...Who maketh the clouds His chariot!
Who walketh upon the wind!
The glory of the Lord shall endure for ever,
The Lord shall rejoice in all His works...
I will sing unto the Lord as long as I shall live!
I will sing praise to my God while I have my being!
Bless thou the Lord, O my soul! Praise ye the Lord!"
(Psalm 104)

The seed of Elijah's sowing was bearing fruit beyond all imagining. It was, indeed, the harvest of the Lord! As the last, wonderful notes melted away into the earth of Israel and Elijah lifted up his arms in final blessing, the enormous crowd, with one accord, swayed to the ground.

"The Lord bless you and keep you.
The Lord make His face to shine upon you
And be gracious unto you.

The Lord lift up the light of His countenance upon you
And give you peace!"
(Numbers 6, 24-26)

It was to be the last and the loveliest message of the great and mighty God of Israel, through Elijah his beloved servant, to His chosen people.

The couch of Ahaziah creaked in dull agony in the fountain court of the Samarian palace. The King dozed fitfully, clutching at shadows in his darkening world. Only the tinkling of the water kept him company; even the dogs had slunk from the steamy smell of death.

Suddenly the waiting noontide caught the far-off noise of the approaching host. Still hidden in the hills, the loudness swelled like the rumble of a nearing storm… or of an attacking army!

"The Syrians are upon us!"

Swiftly the rumour spread. "The gates! The guard!"

"Man the defences… Baal curse those Aramaeans!"

"Sound the alarm!"

Then the first of the long procession wound into the valley and the life of Elijah came, at last, full circle.

Old and travel-stained as he was, the prophet seemed to tower above the sick-bed. The King made one feeble attempt to bolster his dying kingship.

"Seize him," he croaked. "Throw him to the dogs!"

But not a man moved and even the fountain seemed to

mock his impotence. Jezebel, behind the lattice screen, curled her rouged lips in a derisive sneer.

"Know then, O king, again I say, the Lord has cursed you where you lie! You, who have called upon the gods of Baal, shall never leave your couch alive!

The God of Israel has nothing more to say. We shall not meet again."

He swung around, scorning the flattery of the Court, and strode, unharmed, through the dead treasure-house, into the living day.

Later, when all the multitude had been dispersed, two silent figures stopped and turned to look back from the crest of Ephraim.

They watched the sun, red as a ball of fire, sink down behind the turrets of Samaria, flooding the towers in weird and bloody light. Then, as the glow retreated slowly into gathering night, the first wails of the mourners in the palace rose to the darkening skies.

Elijah, resting now upon Elisha's arm, heard too, within his heart, his own, quiet summons to be gone…

Chapter 12

ELIJAH'S FINAL JOURNEY

IT WAS SO LIKE ELIJAH that his final journey should be as unassuming as the man himself.

Yet, for those who loved and followed him, his path directed on a course that all might easily understand. From his resting place at Gilgal, he set out towards the gates of heaven. So had Jacob recognised the spot his head had lodged upon, at Bethel, and dreamed he saw a ladder linking heaven and earth, a path for all who loved the Lord and did His bidding… For his departing descendant too, it now became the gateway to his journey to the stars!

The faithful company who kept the shrine read the message of Elijah's arrival immediately. But both the prophets appeared so undisturbed at death's approach that the priests took Elisha on one side and tactfully warned him of Elijah's coming end.

Elisha gave them short shrift,

"As if I, his keeper and his son, did not know this thing that is to be," he chided them. "You talk as though it is a matter to be dreaded. Hold your peace! Can you not see our father is teaching us one last and vital lesson—that death is a friend and not an enemy, when it is but a stairway up to heaven?"

Elijah returned from the tabernacle.

"Elisha, my son, now we must say goodbye. Our God is calling me and where I go you may not follow."

But Elisha was adamant. Nothing was going to stop him attending on his master while he remained on earth.

"As the Lord liveth, and as thy soul liveth, I will not leave thee!"

So the two of them turned their faces eastwards and took the long, winding road down from the hills onto the plains of Jordan.

How different from the sun-dried slopes and silver olive groves of Bethel! Here was the luxuriance of Jericho with its cool spring and waving palm trees. The travellers were more than glad to reach it across the oppressive heat of the surrounding Jordan plain.

Again Elijah's unspoken message was spelt out by Elisha: Death was a door, a welcome victory, a loving call from God to return home. Indeed, Jericho, with its lush of green and its wealth of fruits, seemed almost like a glimpse of heaven itself…

Elisha tended his master for the last time, pouring the water to wash the dust from off his hands and feet, combing his hair and tempting him to eat. The picture of his care and love carried down the years to stamp him, decades later, as "The one who had poured water on Elijah's hands"... A kindly epitaph and well deserved.

Nor was he again put off by Elijah's prayer that he stay there and rest.

"No father, as thy soul shall live, I will not leave thee now."

So the two friends, watched from the sanctuary by the silent company of the priests and prophets, walked through the gates of Jericho... the gates, indeed, of Joshua's Promised Land... and upstream to the ford of Joshua's crossing.

The map of history rolled itself back once more, as the mantle of Elijah caused the waters to divide and they crossed dry-shod, two frail, diminishing figures, and were lost so soon from sight among the tamarisks upon the farther bank.

Suddenly Elijah stopped, firming his staff, and turned to his companion.

"Elisha, dearer to me than a son, what can a father's blessing leave with you?"

Elisha caught a glimpse of the lonely path that opened out before him, his life without Elijah's staff to guide, his wisdom to direct... Catching the kindly hand, he clutched it hard.

"Leave me the portion of the eldest son, my father. For without your eyes, how shall I see? Without your ears, how hear? Without your wisdom, how direct the path of Israel?

Leave me thy spirit, doubly blessed, that God may ever be within my heart and in my understanding."

Elijah understood and gravely answered:

"That is a portion only God can give, my son, but I will indeed ask this of His Mercy and His Love..." He paused, listening, as was his wont. "Know then, that if, as I am taken up, your eyes can bear the sight, then is the Spirit of the Living God bestowed on you in all its majesty and power.

"Nor I, nor anyone, can size the fitness of your prayer, save only God."

They walked again. The way led gently up between the valley sides where pomegranate trees dabbled their toes in dilettante streams and fig trees, with outstretched fingers, blessed the gardens in their shade. The voices of the travellers, as they passed, settled in murmurs into the peacefulness.

Then the green curtain suddenly swung aside and the fierce backcloth of the Moab mountains seared their horizon! The world fell away behind them as they climbed through purple chasms into a giant place of soaring crags and hollow echoings. At length they stood upon the crowning ridge and met the ribbon road, as ancient as the memories of the hills, the Highway of the Kings.

Even as they reached the road, a mighty wind swept them apart. A sudden, brilliant light dazzled Elisha's eyes. Out of the blinding sand a flaming chariot sprang into the air, drawn by unearthly horses...

He heard his anguished cry:

"Father, my father! The strength of Israel and all her chariots and steeds...!"

Elijah, on the threshold of the Great Beyond, also had heard the drumming of the hooves, the thunder of the messengers of God. But perhaps, within the wind, the Still, Small Voice still whispered for his ear alone.

For him alone may we not dream an even gentler message?

Did two strong arms, perhaps, lift him from out the fiery cloud and set him up behind a proud, curved neck?

And in his ear and in his heart... a well-remembered Voice:

"How merciful is our God upon His throne! Welcome, Elijah, brother of my soul!"

And as the glory of the Lord dissolved into the desert air, a tattered, camel cloak drifted down out of the settling dust. Down to Elisha's feet, without a sound, to fold itself upon the last and loveliest miracle of the Lord, the God of Israel, for Elijah who was His servant and His friend.

AFTERWORD

HERE IS A NEW APPROACH to an old and well-loved Bible story. Elijah has come alive!

But he may not fit in with the image that many people have cherished of him until now.

The Holy Bible has, among its most shrewd characteristics, the ability to lull one into a feeling of safe over-familiarity with its verses. Then, one day, it deals you a suddenly unmistakable blow between the eyes when you are re-reading a particular line which you have taken for granted a hundred times before.

I experienced such an awakening a while ago when I was reading the account of the transfiguration of Jesus.

"His raiment was white and glistening, and behold, there talked with Him two men, which were Moses and Elijah!" (Luke 9:30) Moses to represent the Law, Elijah personifying the Prophets.

To begin with, of course, the whole thing is rather confused since "Elijah" is written as "Elias" and, at a superficial reading, one might be forgiven for mistaking him for Isaiah, "Esaias" in the New Testament. But how wrong you would be! The man was none other than Elijah, no doubt still in his leather girdle and his cloak and thus instantly recognisable to the disciples. And here he was, one of the only two figures from the whole of the history of the Jews, to be deemed fit, in the eyes of heaven, to commune with the Son of God in all His glory!

Now the history of the Jewish race is so thick with heroes and prophets that there is almost an embarrassment of riches from which to choose. There is Isaiah with a stupendous double book after his name. There is David, the beloved of the Lord, Abraham the father of the chosen People, Jacob, Jeremiah... the list is endless.

But of all these, it suddenly dawned on me that, of all the prophets, it was only Elijah who had been chosen to meet with Jesus.

Moses, as representing the Law, one could easily accept. For he it was who received the original Ten Commandments upon Mount Sinai and indeed his achievements and personality do tower uniquely in the Old Testament. They occupy four long books. But the more I thought about it, the more I had to admit that, somewhere along the line of my Bible study, I had most woefully overlooked the importance of that second chosen personality, representing the prophets, Elijah.

So I turned back to read, and as I read and re-read, the story of Elijah began to glow in a very new and exciting light. Not only did he gradually become a completely alive and real person, but he also grew into a supremely lovable and delightful human being. As humble, in his way, as his great hero, Moses.

I think it was this very ingrained humility of his that had caught me out in the first place. I get the strong impression in fact, that Elijah is almost deliberately effacing himself in the pages of the history of the kings of Israel so that only those of sincere and honourable intent might even begin to discover his true identity.

He is certainly like that in the few chapters that cover his life. He appears and disappears again in the most extraordinary way, almost as though he were playing hide and seek with you or leading you on...

He led me on! And what a journey it became!

For I plunged headlong into the fabulous and hair-raising story of the Northern Kingdom, at the very heart of which is the life and death struggle between Elijah and the infamous Queen Jezebel for the soul of Israel. As a drama it is equal to anything in the history of the Jewish People, or of many other people, come to that. All of which is played out among the fascinating and hallowed scenery of the Holy Land, under a blazing sun and the brilliant blue of the Mediterranean sky!

Then in the end, the whole scene goes up in flames before our eyes as the body and soul of Elijah roar off in a blaze of glory on the wings of the messengers of the Almighty, the Lord of Hosts!

The end of his life is then as enigmatic as its beginning. I further made the discovery that the chosen people had accepted that he had never died at all. Always, deep down, it became clear that they still cherished this memory of his great love for them. Always they looked for his return as the coming Shepherd who would lead them home…

You can trace their longing in rare glimpses in the Old Testament until it bursts out in undisguised eagerness in the final, beautiful chapter of the Book of Malachi which closes the ancient scriptures in a paean of glory and of promise:
"But unto you that fear My Name shall the Sun of Righteousness arise with healing in His wings!... Behold! I will send you Elijah, the prophet, before the coming of the great and dreadful Day of the Lord. And he shall turn the hearts of the fathers to the children and the hearts of the children to the fathers. . ."

It swells out as the finale on a mighty organ and the note it ends on is… Elijah!

Not surprisingly then, it is this note too that heralds the next and greatest act in the history of the Jews and, indeed, the world. The flag-bearer for the Christ, the Saviour, can only be the expected Elijah re-incarnated… and it is!

So sings the Angel of the Lord to the astonished Zacharias when he brings the glad news of his long-awaited son:

"He will go… in the spirit and the power of Elijah." (Luke 1: 17) And John the Baptist stands before us, the very image of his prophetic predecessor.

So long had they treasured the picture of the gaunt Elijah in their hearts that all Israel recognised him on sight. He was clothed in rough camel-hair, the girdle of tough leather about his loins and he thrived on the diet of the wilderness, the honey of wild bees and the black pods of the locust tree. It was Elijah, in person!

Jesus himself set the seal on his reality: "John is Elijah, whose coming was prophesied." (Matt. 2: 14.)

Later on, when John the Baptist had become himself a legend of the past, people were still clinging to his image. When Jesus enquired who he was generally considered to be among his countrymen, the disciples disclosed that most people still thought of him as either John the Baptist... or the prophet Elijah! (Mark 8:28.)... And so we come to the place where I personally first met and recognised the true Elijah, at the Transfiguration.

It is a story, like all immortal tales, without an end and its hero, living through generation after generation in the hearts of Israel, never dies.

And still today, at the yearly Jewish celebration of their Passover, is the door left open for his coming, and an extra cup of wine poured out, for the long-awaited return of their beloved prophet of all time, the great Elijah!

Printed in Great Britain
by Amazon